*Jane Austen's*

# Sense

## &

# *Sensibility*

**adapted for the stage**
**by**
## Paula K. Parker

WordCrafts

**WordCrafts Theatrical Press**

Published by WordCrafts Theatrical Press
912 E. Lincoln St.
Tullahoma, TN 37388
www.wordcrafts.net

*Jane Austen's*

# Sense

&

# Sensibility

adapted for the stage
by

# Paula K. Parker

# Playwright's Notes
## on Staging
## Jane Austen's Sense & Sensibility

**Jane Austen's Sense & Sensibility** is wonderful character-driven story that may be played with understated nuance on a minimalistic set. But it is also a marvelous period piece that lends itself to gorgeous costumes and magnificent sets. I've attempted to write the play so that it can be produced on a variety of stages by theatres with either large or small budgets.

I believe it is the responsibility of the playwright to write the play, and that it is the responsibility of the director to direct the play. As such, I have refrained from inserting many stage directions, and grant the director the freedom and license to direct the show as he or she sees fit.

One note I thought important to include regards the significant prop - the pianoforte. Although theatre companies who have access to a piano and wish to use it may certainly do so. The pianoforte, however, was not a piano; it was a precursor of the modern day piano. It was much smaller and lighter, and in many cases resembled a rectangular desk. A simulated pianoforte, faced away from the audience, would be quite suitable for this production and would certainly be easier for scene changes.

Blessings,

Paula K. Parker

# <u>Characters</u>
## In Order of Appearance

Thomas, the butler at Norland
John Dashwood
Fanny Dashwood, John's wife
Mrs. Dashwood
Margaret Dashwood
Marianne Dashwood
Elinor Dashwood
Edward Ferrars,
Cook
Sir John Middleton
Mrs. Jennings
Butler at Barton Hall
Colonel Brandon
Mr. Willoughby
Butler at Delaford
Mrs. (Charlotte) Palmer
Mr. Palmer
Lucy Steele
Express Rider
Johnson, Mrs. Jennings' Butler
Miss Grey – this character has no lines
Mr. Robert Ferrars
The Doctor

# ACT I

## Scene 1

SETTING:              A parlor at Norland.

AT RISE:              **THOMAS** ushers **JOHN** and **FANNY**
                      **DASHWOOD** into the room.

### THOMAS
If you would be so good as to wait in here, Mrs. Dashwood, Mr.
Dashwood, I will inform Mrs. Dashwood of your arrival.

### JOHN
And you say that my stepmother has not yet left her rooms?
What of my sisters?

### THOMAS
No, Sir, Mrs. Dashwood has not yet left her rooms. As for the
young ladies, I understand that Miss Dashwood is visiting
someone in the village who is sick; she informed Cook not to
expect her for luncheon. Miss Marianne and Miss Margaret had
Cook prepare them a picnic meal and are spending the morning
on the far side of Norland, sketching.

### FANNY
Really?

### JOHN
Thank you, Thomas.

(**THOMAS** bows and exits.)

### FANNY

Still in her rooms? At this hour? John, what must your
stepmother be thinking? And your sisters to be absent from the
house when we were expected?

### JOHN

My dear Fanny, it has not even been a week since my father
died. My stepmother's grief is understandable. As for my sisters,
we cannot fault them that fine traveling weather allowed us to
arrive earlier than expected.

>           (**JOHN** sits while **FANNY** wanders around the
>           room, picking up items to inspect them.)

### FANNY

I would think they would be waiting since dawn to greet you
with open arms. After all, you plan to be more than generous
with them. I still do not understand this most unusual situation,
John; what must have your father been thinking in his request of
you?

### JOHN

My dear, I've explained it before. Norland belonged to my
father's uncle. My mother died when I was quite young. My
father remarried and he and his new wife had three daughters. As
his uncle had no heirs, the old gentleman invited Father and his
new family to live at Norland. After his uncle's death, Father
learned that - while the will allowed for he and his family to
continue living at Norland throughout his lifetime - upon
Father's death, the entire estate would pass to me. Nothing in
Uncle's will allowed for Father to provide for his wife and
daughters. It was my father's last request to me that I should
assist his widow and daughters.

### FANNY

He did not know what he was talking of, I dare say. Ten to one
he was light headed at the time, my dear John, to suggest that

you give away half of your fortune. What will we live upon? We barely have enough now to support Norland and our house in town and my brother Edward will be arriving here in less than a fortnight.

**JOHN**
Fanny, we are not as bad as all that. Father did not stipulate for any particular sum; he only requested me, in general terms, to assist them. As he required the promise, I could not do less than give it. I was thinking three thousand pounds. Something must be done for them whenever they leave Norland.

**FANNY**
Well, then, let something be done for them. But consider that when the money is once parted with, it never can return. Your sisters will marry and it will be gone forever.

**JOHN**
Well…perhaps, it would be better if the sum were halved…five hundred pounds apiece would be a prodigious increase to their fortunes.

**FANNY**
What brother would do half so much for his real sisters?

**JOHN**
I would not wish to do anything *mean*. One had rather, on such occasions, do too much than too little. No one, at least, can think I have not done enough for them; even *they* can hardly expect more.

**FANNY**
There is no knowing what *they* may expect; but the question is, what can you afford to do?

**JOHN**
I think I may afford to give them five hundred pounds apiece. As it is, the girls will each have above three thousand pounds on their mother's death – a very comfortable fortune.

**FANNY**
To be sure it is. If they marry, they will be sure of doing well; and if they do not, they may all live very comfortably together on the interest of the ten thousand pounds.

> (**THOMAS** enters, carrying a tea tray. He places it on a table and bows.)

**THOMAS**
Ma'am, Sir, Mrs. Dashwood's maid informed me that Mrs. Dashwood is lying down with a prodigious head ache and cannot arise from her bed. Mrs. Dashwood desired me to convey her apologies over not being able to greet you and to assure you that she looks forward to seeing you at supper. She instructed me to have your things taken to your rooms. I brought in some refreshment while your rooms are readied.

**JOHN**
Thank you, Thomas.

> (**THOMAS** bows and exits. **FANNY** crosses to pour out tea for her and **JOHN**.)

**JOHN**
As I think upon it, I believe you are right, my dear. The girls will surely be well provided for in marriage. I do not know whether it would not be more advisable to do something for my stepmother while she lives rather than for the girls. Something of an annuity; my sisters would benefit from it as well. A hundred a year would make them all perfectly comfortable.

**FANNY**
To be sure, it is better than parting with fifteen hundred all at once. But then, if Mrs. Dashwood should live fifteen years, we shall completely be taken in. If you observe, my dear, people always live forever when there is an annuity to be paid them.

**JOHN**
I believe you are right, my love…it would be better if I occasionally give them assistance. A gift of fifty pounds now and then will prevent their ever being distressed for money and will, I think, amply discharge my promise to my father.

**FANNY**
To be sure it will. Indeed, to say the truth, I am convinced within myself that your father had no idea of your giving them any money at all. I daresay the assistance your father thought of would involve you looking for a comfortable house, helping them move their things, and sending them presents of fish and vegetables when they are in season. Altogether they will have five hundred a year amongst them and what on earth can four women want for more than that? They will have no carriage, no horses and hardly any servants; they will keep no company and can have no expenses of any kind. Only consider how comfortable they will be. They will be much more able to give *you* something.

**JOHN**
Fish and vegetables, you say? Hmmmm….upon my word, my dear Fanny, I believe you are perfectly right. Fish and vegetables…yes, I believe you are right.

**(BLACK OUT)**

# ACT I

## Scene 2

SETTING:            The same parlor at Norland, a
                    month later.

AT RISE:            **MRS. DASHWOOD, MARIANNE**
                    and **MARGARET** are sitting. **MRS.
                    DASHWOOD** is doing needlework
                    while **MARGARET** reads aloud to
                    **MARIANNE**.

### MARGARET
(Stumbles through the reading without much
feeling. **MARIANNE** grows agitated as
**MARGARET** reads.)
Harp of the North, farewell! The hills grow dark,
On purple peaks a deeper shade descending;
In twilight copse the glow-worm lights her spark,
The deer, half-seen, are to the covert wending.
Resume thy wizard elm!

### MARIANNE
No, no, no! Do not read it thus. There is no feeling, no passion.

### MARGARET
I care not. They are merely words.

### MARIANNE
(Grows angrier as she speaks.)
Merely words? Merely words? How can you say that? This is Sir
Walter Scott, not one of your travel guide books.

**MRS. DASHWOOD**
Girls, please. Marianne, lower your voice. Margaret, please do as your sister asks.

**MARGARET**
But, Mama, I cannot read as Marianne desires.

**MARIANNE**
Read it thus;
                    (Reads fluently, with great emotion.)
Harp of the North, farewell! The hills grow dark,
On purple peaks a deeper shade descending;
In twilight copse the glow-worm lights her spark,
The deer, half-seen, are to the covert wending.
Resume thy wizard elm!

Now please try again.

**MARGARET**
Harp of the North, farewell! The hills grow dark,
On purple peaks a deeper shade descending;

**MARIANNE**
That was much better.

                    (**ELINOR** and **EDWARD FERRARS** enter.
                    They are dressed for a walk)

**MRS. DASHWOOD**
There you are, Elinor. Oh, good morning, Mr. Ferrars.

**ELINOR**
Hello, Mama

**EDWARD**
    (Bows to ladies.)
Good morning, Mrs. Dashwood. Miss Marianne. Miss Margaret.

**MARGARET**
Good morning Edward. You look pretty, Elinor.

**ELINOR**
Thank you, Margaret. I am walking to the village to arrange the altar flowers at the church and Edward has offered to escort me. He has expressed a desire to speak with Reverend Taylor.

**EDWARD**
I would like to discuss the Church with him. I have often thought I would enjoy the life of a clergyman.

**MRS. DASHWOOD**
I'm sure you would make an excellent minister, Mr. Ferrars.

**EDWARD**
Thank you.

**ELINOR**
We will be back in time for luncheon, Mama.

**MRS. DASHWOOD**
That's fine. Have a wonderful time and pray convey my regards to Reverend Taylor.

    (Ad lib, good byes and bows. **ELINOR** and
    **EDWARD** exit and begin walking across the
    stage. The remaining Dashwood ladies *chat*
    while **ELINOR** and **EDWARD** talk.)

**EDWARD**
Ah…what a beautiful morning. Norland is a beautiful estate,
Miss Dashwood. I could easily make my visit an extended one.

**ELINOR**
Thank you, Mr. Ferrars. I have always loved it here. I hope
Fanny and John will come to love it as well.

**EDWARD**
I cannot imagine how they could not. A handsome and
comfortable home, well-tended gardens. And the people I have
met thus far are quite pleasant; what more can they ask for?

**ELINOR**
Living here is all I have ever wanted. I do not think I would
enjoy living in London.

**EDWARD**
If I could find a home in the country, I would be most content.

**ELINOR**
Perhaps you could ask Reverend Taylor; he might know of a
living that is available.

**EDWARD**
I do appreciate your offer to introduce me to Reverend Taylor,
Miss Dashwood.

**ELINOR**
You are more than welcome, Mr. Ferrars. I think you will like
him. He is a kind-hearted man who cares about the people in his
church. What is more, he makes the stories from scripture come
alive. When he tells the story of the Garden of Eden or David
standing against Goliath, I can almost see it.

**EDWARD**
You are fortunate, indeed. My experience with clergyman is quite the opposite; very stodgy, with much doom and gloom in their sermons. Always pronouncing more 'don'ts' than 'dos' upon their parishioners. I dreaded attended services as a young boy.

**ELINOR**
With such exposure, I am surprised you wish to enter the Church.

**EDWARD**
But it is for that very reason I wish to become a clergyman. Attending services should be a lightness and joy into people's week and giving them hope and strength for the coming days.

**ELINOR**
That is exactly how I feel about attending services.

**EDWARD**
I confess I am not surprised, Miss Dashwood. The more I get to know you, the more I find a kindred spirit, which is a rare find. Few in my family understand my desires in this area.

**ELINOR**
I know what you mean, Mr. Ferrars. My mother and sisters comment frequently on my desire to arrange flowers for the altar or visiting the sick in the village. In fact, if Reverend Taylor were not already married, and over twice my age, I am certain some construe my actions as an attempt to woo him.
(laughs)

**EDWARD**
I could understand their reasoning, Miss Dashwood. I confess I think you would be the perfect choice of a clergyman's wife.

(She pauses and looks at him. He smiles. They
exit the stage. The dialogue among the
remaining Dashwood ladies resumes.)

**MARIANNE**
Edward wants to be a minister!? Could anything more be needed
to render him a complete bore?

**MRS. DASHWOOD**
Marianne Dashwood! What a thing to say! Mr. Ferrars is a
gentleman.

**MARIANNE**
I did not imply that Edward was ungentlemanly. I said he was a
complete bore.

**MARGARET**
Edward is not a complete bore. He spent a whole morning telling
me about his travels to Spain and Italy.

**MARIANNE**
Edward might be everything that is desired in a gentleman,
Mama, but he has no passion. I do not understand him at all. I
know he has talked to you about his travels, Margaret, but I do
not understand how Elinor can consent to spend time with him.
They have been together almost continually since his arrival a
fortnight ago.

**MRS. DASHWOOD**
You exaggerate, Marianne; although Elinor and Edward have
spent time in each other's company, it has not been continual. As
for understanding him, it is enough for me that he is unlike his
sister, Fanny. To me, that implies everything amiable. In fact,
after observing Elinor and Edward together these past weeks, I
am convinced that in a few months time, Elinor will in all
probability be settled for life.

**MARIANNE**
What? Do you mean…married?! Elinor and Edward?

**MRS. DASHWOOD**
Do you disapprove of your sister's choice?

**MARIANNE**
Edward is very amiable, I agree…but yet…there is something wanting. His figure is not striking, his eyes want that spirit, that fire, and I'm afraid he has no real artistic taste. Music seems scarcely to attract him, he does not appear to understand paintings and as for poetry…how spiritless, how tame was Edward's manner in reading to us last night. Your reading was vastly superior to his, Margaret.

**MRS. DASHWOOD**
Elinor has not your feelings, Marianne. I'm sure she would be happy with him.

**MARIANNE**
Happy. The more I know of the world, the more am I convinced that I shall never see a man whom I can really love.

(**FANNY** enters.)

**FANNY**
Good morning, Mrs. Dashwood. Marianne. Margaret.

(**MRS. DASHWOOD, MARIANNE**, and **MARGARET** stand. All curtsies)

**MRS. DASHWOOD**
Good morning, Fanny. Will you sit with us?

**FANNY**
Thank you, but I cannot. I am writing my mother and must
consult with Edward on a particular question. Thomas thought
perhaps he was in here, telling Miss Margaret about yet another
of his trips.

(**MRS. DASHWOOD, MARIANNE** and
**MARGARET** look at each other.)

**MARIANNE**
If you will excuse us, Fanny; Margaret and I were just about to
walk to the woods.

**MARGARET**
We were?

(**MARIANNE** takes **MARGARET'S** hand.)

**MARIANNE**
Yes, we were. Goodbye Mama, Fanny. We will be back by
luncheon, Mama.

(They curtsey and exit.)

**MRS. DASHWOOD**
You must forgive Marianne's sudden departure. I'm certain she
wanted to grant us private conversation…about your brother
Edward.

**FANNY**
Indeed? And what would we have to discuss about Edward that
warrants privacy? Is something amiss?

**MRS. DASHWOOD**
No, indeed. Truth to tell, he was here several minutes ago; but he
has left to escort Elinor to the church in the village. I understand

he wishes to enter the Church...If my husband were still alive, he would speak with Edward...I wish to assure you...my girls and I have been quite happy since Edward arrived...we are...quite fond of him.

> (**FANNY** stares at **MRS. DASHWOOD** for a moment and then gives a light, yet sarcastic laugh.)

### FANNY
My dear, Mrs. Dashwood, Edward may *wish* as he chooses; but our mother has great expectations of both he and our younger brother, Robert, distinguishing themselves. She is resolved that they enter politics or become connected with some great man...As for marriage, Mother is equally resolved that they marry well...It can be difficult for young men like Edward and Robert...there are so many...undeserving...young women who try to draw them in.

> (The two women stare at each other for several moments.)

### MRS. DASHWOOD
I completely understand you.

> (**MRS. DASHWOOD** curtsies and exits. **FANNY** watches her leave and turns towards the audience with an evil smile.)

### (BLACKOUT)

# ACT I

## Scene 3

SETTING:          The same parlor at Norland, several
                  weeks later.

AT RISE:          **ELINOR** and **MARIANNE** enter, with
                  **THOMAS** behind,  carrying a tea tray.
                  He sets the tray on a side table.

#### THOMAS
Will there be anything else, Miss Dashwood? Shall I pour out for
you?

#### ELINOR
No, thank you, Thomas. The others will be here soon; we shall
wait for them. Please let Cook know that she has once again
outdone herself.

#### THOMAS
Yes, Miss.

                  (**THOMAS** bows and exits.)

                  (**ELINOR** crosses to adjust an arrangement of
                  flowers. **MARIANNE** follows.)

#### MARIANNE
Edward is a…very amiable gentleman.

#### ELINOR
He is indeed.

#### MARIANNE
You have spent considerable time with him since he arrived at
Norland.

**ELINOR**

Yes, he and I have been thrown together a good deal.

**MARIANNE**

I think he is…everything that is worthy and amiable.

**ELINOR**

I'm sure his dearest friends could not be dissatisfied with such a commendation…I have enjoyed our time together. I find his mind is well formed,  the expressions of his eyes uncommonly good, and the general expression of his countenance to be sweet.

**MARIANNE**

Well formed? Uncommonly good? A sweet countenance? With such praise, I shall very soon think him handsome. When you tell me to love him as a brother, I shall consider him perfect. Oh, Elinor, how shall I do without you?

**ELINOR**

Do without me? What can you mean? I do not attempt to deny that I think very highly of him…that I greatly esteem…that I like him…

**MARIANNE**

Esteem him! Like him! Oh, cold-hearted, Elinor! Use those words again and I will leave this room.

**ELINOR**

I mean no offense in speaking of my feelings. Believe them to be stronger than I have declared, that there is hope of his affection for me, but further than this you must *not* believe.

> (**MRS. DASHWOOD, MARGARET, JOHN, FANNY**, and **EDWARD** enter. General ad-lib greetings. **FANNY** sits behind the tea table to

pour out. **ELINOR** hands around teacups, while **MARGARET** offers a plate of tea biscuits.)

**MRS. DASHWOOD**
I received a correspondence from Sir John Middleton today.

**JOHN**
*Sir* John Middleton?

**MRS. DASHWOOD**
He is a relative of mine. He wrote to say that he understood that we were in need of a dwelling and has offered to let us have the cottage on his estate, Barton Park.

**JOHN**
Where is Barton Park located? I hope it is not far from Norland.

**MRS. DASHWOOD**
It's in Devonshire.

(General exclamations.)

**EDWARD**
Devonshire? So far? Surely you do not mean to accept his offer?

**MRS. DASHWOOD**
I'm afraid we must, Edward. We cannot continue to impose on John and Fanny's generosity.

**JOHN**
When do you mean to move to Devonshire?

**MRS. DASHWOOD**
As soon as arrangements may be made.

**FANNY**

A cottage? How quaint. If we didn't have Norland and our house in town, I should love to live in a cottage. I'm sure it will be quite tidy and snug.

**MARGARET**

You will come to visit us, will you not, Edward?

**MRS. DASHWOOD**

Although it is but a cottage, I hope to see many of my friends there. Indeed, Edward, you would be most welcome at any time.

**EDWARD**

Thank you, Mrs. Dashwood; I will indeed plan on a visit. Soon.

**FANNY**

Edward, did I mention the correspondence I received from Mother? She writes that she needs you in town immediately for some business that requires your presence. She believes you will be in town for an indeterminate time.

**MRS. DASHWOOD**

Whenever you are free, then, Edward…Sir John insists that we not concern ourselves over furniture, as the cottage is completely furnished. However, there are certain pieces of sentimental attachment here at Norland.

**MARIANNE**

The pianoforte…

**FANNY**

My dear Miss Marianne, that pianoforte belongs…

(**MRS. DASHWOOD** interrupts her.)

**MRS. DASHWOOD**
…to Marianne. It was a gift from my mother to me when I was a girl and I gave it to Marianne when she showed proficiency on it.

(**FANNY** is speechless.)

**MRS. DASHWOOD**
After I wrote Sir John, I spoke with the servants. Thomas and Cook have indicated their desire to go with us to Devonshire.

**JOHN**
Thomas? And Cook?

**MRS. DASHWOOD**
Yes.

**FANNY**
But we cannot manage without a butler or cook.

**MRS. DASHWOOD**
I'm sure you'll soon find someone to replace them. In the meantime, Cook assures me that the scullery maid Betty shows promise in the kitchen and that she makes a sumptuous dish of fish and vegetables.

**JOHN**
Fish?

**FANNY**
And vegetables?

(**BLACKOUT**)

# ACT I

## Scene 4

SETTING:              Several weeks later. The parlor in
                      Barton Cottage.

AT RISE:              **MRS. DASHWOOD, ELINOR,**
                      **MARIANNE** and **MARGARET** enter.

#### MARIANNE
Here at last! I thought we would never arrive.

#### MARGARET
I am going to explore!

#### MRS. DASHWOOD
And I am going to sit in a chair that isn't moving.
                      (She removes her cloak and crosses to a chair to
                      sit.)

#### ELINOR
Darling, please begin your explorations in the kitchen and let
Cook and Thomas know we have arrived.

#### MARGARET
I will.
                      (She exits.)

                      (**MARIANNE** and **ELINOR** remove their
                      cloaks and gloves. **ELINOR** crosses to a
                      table to inspect a stack of envelopes.
                      **MARIANNE** crosses to the window to stare
                      outside.)

**MRS. DASHWOOD**
Well, this appears to be a comfortable room.

**MARIANNE**
But as a cottage, it is defective. The building is regular and the roof tiled. The window shutters are not painted green, nor are the outer walls covered with honeysuckles.

**ELINOR**
Tragedy indeed. Mama, it appears that John collected our correspondence that arrived for us at Norland and sent them on.
>                   (She hands the stack of envelopes to her
>                   mother.)

>                   (**MARGARET** enters with **THOMAS** and
>                   **COOK**, both of whom are carrying trays of
>                   food. They set the trays down and bow/curtsey.)

**MRS. DASHWOOD**
Thomas. Cook. It is good to see both of you again.

**THOMAS**
If I may be so bold, it is good to see you, Ma'am and the young ladies. We arrived early this morning and have been awaiting you since luncheon. When the wagon arrived with your boxes half an hour ago, Cook and I knew you wouldn't be too far behind.

**COOK**
It was then I popped a pan of strawberry tarts into the oven.

**MARGARET**
Strawberry tarts!
>                   (She hurries to the tray of food.)

**COOK**
I suspected Miss Margaret would be pleased to see them. And there was a prodigious amount of strawberries in the basket of food Sir John Middleton sent over this morning.

**MRS. DASHWOOD**
Sir John sent a basket of food?

**THOMAS**
He did indeed, filled with vegetables from his kitchen garden and fruit from his orchards. He told Cook not to worry about trying to plant so late in the season and to send over to Barton Park for whatever she needed.

> (SOUND EFFECT: The noise of a carriage arriving. **MARGARET** runs to look out the 'front window')

**MARGARET**
A carriage has arrived, Mama. A gentlemen and a lady are getting out.
> (She laughs as **THOMAS** exits to answer the door.)

He is wearing a powdered wig and she is wearing *such* a hat!

**COOK**
The gentleman is Sir John. The lady is Mrs. Jennings, his late wife's mother. Mrs. Jennings divides her time between London and Barton Hall.

**ELINOR**
What an advantage to have sent you and Thomas ahead; we have all the local gossip without any effort on our part.
> (They all laugh.)

(**THOMAS** enters and bows)

**THOMAS**
Mrs. Jennings and Sir John Middleton.

(**MRS. JENNINGS** and **SIR JOHN** enter. The
**DASHWOOD LADIES** stand. Bows/curtsies.
**THOMAS** and **COOK** exit.)

**SIR JOHN**
Here you are at last! Mother and I have been waiting for you all
morning. I saw your carriage drive past Barton Park and
wondered why you didn't stop.

**MRS. JENNINGS**
I told John that I suspected you were fatigued from your journey
and wanted to see your new home.

**SIR JOHN**
So I said, "Mother, let's go make their acquaintance and
welcome them to Devonshire."

**MRS. JENNINGS**
And so here we are. But, where are our manners, Sir John? We
have rambled on without proper introductions.

**SIR JOHN**
Pray forgive me, Mrs. Dashwood. This is Mrs. Jennings, my
mother-in-law.

**MRS. DASHWOOD**
How do you do? These are my daughters, Elinor, Marianne, and
Margaret.

**MRS. JENNINGS**

How do you do? I feel as if I know you already. You'll all such beauties! I am certain when news of your arrival gets around, we will have no peace at Barton Park. Which is exactly as we like it, is it not, Sir John?

**SIR JOHN**

It is indeed, Mother. Nothing is more delightful than to have company every evening. In fact, why don't you plan to dine at Barton Park tonight? I'm sure your servants haven't had time to set up the kitchen to their liking.

**MRS. DASHWOOD**

I wouldn't want to presume…

**SIR JOHN**

No presumption at all…in fact…what think you, Mother? I heard that Colonel Brandon was back from town. Do you think he could be persuaded to dine with us?

**MRS. DASHWOOD**

Does Colonel Brandon have a wife?

**MRS. JENNINGS**

No, he does not. If you are thinking of your daughters, I assure you, he is not a confirmed bachelor. As I understand it, in his youth Brandon was passionately in love with a young woman. However, his family did not approve of her. Being the younger son, he was sent into the army; as for the young woman, rumor has it she came to a bad end.

**SIR JOHN**

 When his elder brother died, Brandon inherited Delaford, where he has lived alone, despite attempts on many a mother's part to introduce him to eligible young ladies.

**MRS. JENNINGS**
However, I'm certain when Brandon learns there will be several
beautiful young ladies present tonight, he will readily accept an
invitation to meet new neighbors. Please say you'll accept, Mrs.
Dashwood. I vow, we won't take 'No' for an answer.

**MRS. DASHWOOD**
Well, I guess I...

**SIR JOHN**
Splendid! Don't worry about transportation. I'll send a carriage
around for you all at seven. Now, Mother, I'm sure the ladies
would like to rest before dressing for the evening.

**MRS. JENNINGS**
Yes indeed. I need to speak to Cook about preparing a
sumptuous meal for our new guests. Is there something particular
that you love? I see Miss Margaret enjoys strawberries; I'll have
Cook prepare something with strawberries; how would you like
that? Well, let's go, Sir John. Good bye until later!

> (**SIR JOHN** and **MRS. JENNINGS** leave ad
> libbing farewells and comments about the
> coming evening. The Dashwood ladies look at
> each other, dumbfounded.)

**ELINOR**
I may have never been to India, but I do believe we have just
experienced what Edward described as a whirling dervish.

**(BLACK OUT)**

# ACT I

## Scene 5

SETTING:            A parlor at Barton Park, that evening.
                    There are chairs on one side of the room
                    and a pianoforte, facing downstage, is
                    on one side of the room.

AT RISE:            **SIR JOHN, MRS. JENNINGS, MRS.
                    DASHWOOD, ELINOR,
                    MARIANNE** and **MARGARET** are
                    seated, drinking tea.

### MRS. DASHWOOD
That was a delightful supper, Sir John. Mrs. Jennings.

### SIR JOHN
Glad you enjoyed it.

### MRS. JENNINGS
I'm certainly glad that Miss Margaret enjoyed Cook's strawberry
pie. I will determine whether there is any left that you may take
back to the cottage.

### MARGARET
Thank you!

### SIR JOHN
I'm sorry it was too late to invite other people for supper.

### MRS. DASHWOOD
Pray do not apologize. We certainly did not expect a party.

**MRS. JENNINGS**
All our friends were otherwise engaged. Colonel Brandon sent word that, although he wouldn't be able to come for supper, he would stop by afterwards. But, we will have a party soon to properly introduce you to our friends. Miss Dashwood, Miss Marianne, I do hope that you have not left your heart behind in Sussex. Did you have any beaus? Ah, I can tell by your blush, Miss Dashwood, that you did. Who is he? You might as well tell me, for I shall winkle it out of you…

**ELINOR**
I assure you, Mrs. Jennings…

**MRS. JENNINGS**
I understand; you are not prepared to announce an engagement yet. I daresay he was the curate of the parish.

**MARGARET**
No, that he is not. He is of no profession at all.

**MARIANNE**
Margaret, you know that all this is an invention of your own; there is no such person in existence.

**MARGARET**
(excited)
Well then, he is lately dead, Marianne, for I am sure there was such a man once, and his name begins with an F.

**MRS. JENNINGS**
An F is it? Let's see…Forthwright…Franklin…

**SIR JOHN**
Farnsworth…Farraday…

**MARIANNE**
>(Stands.)

Sir John, may I play your pianoforte?

**SIR JOHN**
>(Startled at her abrupt request.)

…well…certainly my dear…

**MRS. JENNINGS**

How delightful.

>(**MARIANNE** crosses to the pianoforte and
>begins playing. Everyone turns to face her. After
>a few moments, **COLONEL BRANDON**
>enters, although no one sees him immediately.
>He pauses, spellbound by **MARIANNE**. **SIR
>JOHN** notices him.)

**SIR JOHN**

Ah Brandon! You've come at last!

**COLONEL BRANDON**

I hope I'm not too late.

**MRS. JENNINGS**

Not at all. We were having tea. You must come and meet our
new neighbors. This is Mrs. Dashwood, Miss Dashwood, Miss
Margaret, and that is Miss Marianne you heard on the pianoforte.

>(bows/curtsies. Everyone sits)

**SIR JOHN**

Brandon has been our closest neighbor since he came back from
India when he inherited Delaford.

**MARGARET**
India? Pray, Colonel Brandon, will you please tell me about it?

**COLONEL BRANDON**
I have a better idea. If you and your mother and sisters – as well as Mrs. Jennings and Sir John - will consent to be my guests at Delaford, I will show you my sketches of the Taj Mahal.

**MARGARET**
Truly?

**COLONEL BRANDON**
Truly.

**SIR JOHN**
Capital idea, Brandon! I daresay that Miss Margaret won't see a better collection of Indian artifacts than yours.

**MRS. DASHWOOD**
How very kind of you, Colonel. We would be most happy to accept your invitation.

**MRS. JENNINGS**
And perhaps we can persuade Miss Marianne to grace us with a song on your pianoforte. You'll not find a more magnificent instrument than Brandon's.

**MARIANNE**
Is it English or Viennese?

**COLONEL BRANDON**
A Viennese. I had the honor of hearing of one Herr Stein's new pianofortes when I was traveling through Augsburg last year and was determined to purchase one for Delaford.

**MARIANNE**
A Viennese! I have never played on one. I understand that
Wolfgang Amadeus Mozart preferred Herr Stein's pianofortes
due to their light touch.

**COLONEL BRANDON**
That is what I too understand.

**SIR JOHN**
I have not heard your pianoforte played in ages, Brandon. And to
hear Miss Marianne play it; that will be a treat indeed.
(To **ELINOR.**)
Do you play the pianoforte, Miss Dashwood?

**ELINOR**
Oh no. Although I had a music master when I was younger, I
never developed proficiency for the instrument. We leave all the
arts to Marianne; she even supervises Margaret's artistic
education as well as her regular lessons.

**MRS. JENNINGS**
Sir John tells me that Colonel Brandon is quite skillful on the
pianoforte, although he has never performed for me. Perhaps
with you here to talk music with him, Miss Marianne, we might
one day hear him play.
(To **SIR JOHN.**)
What think you, Sir John? Can our Miss Marianne persuade
Brandon to perform a duet?

**SIR JOHN**
Yes…yes…I think she can.
(**SIR JOHN** and **MRS. JENNINGS** laugh, much to the
embarrassment of everyone else.)

**(BLACKOUT.)**

# ACT I

## Scene 6

SETTING:            The parlor at Barton Cottage the next
                    day. (SOUND EFFECT: rain)

AT RISE:            **MRS. DASHWOOD** and **ELINOR** are
                    unpacking a box of pictures and
                    decorations.

### MRS. DASHWOOD
I must say that Sir John and Mrs. Jennings promise to be kind
and attentive neighbors.

### ELINOR
Yes indeed. It appears to be their intention to provide us with
plenty of vegetables, fruit…and husbands.

### MRS. DASHWOOD
Elinor!

### ELINOR
                    (Laughs gently.)
Come Mama, you cannot deny that Mrs. Jennings was obviously
planning a match between Marianne and Colonel Brandon. Not
that she did not give us fair warning. Once Colonel Brandon
arrived at Barton Park, she never ceased trying to throw him and
Marianne together.

(**MRS. DASHWOOD** hesitates and then laughs with
**ELINOR**.)

**MRS. DASHWOOD**

It was rather awkward. Marianne was quite upset.

**ELINOR**

Upset? I am surprised that Marianne was able to hold her tongue until we got home. Do you remember what she said?

> (Impersonates Marianne in an exaggerated manner.)

"But at least, you cannot deny the absurdity of it. Colonel Brandon is so *old*. When is a man to be safe from such as Mrs. Jennings, if age and infirmity will not protect him?"

When I commented on Colonel Brandon having use of all his limbs, she responded,

> (Impersonates Marianne.)

"Did you not hear him complain of the rheumatism? Is not that the commonest infirmity of declining life? And he spoke of flannel waistcoats, which are invariably connected with the aches and pains that afflict the old and feeble!"

**MRS. DASHWOOD**

At this rate you girls must be in continual terror of my decay. It must seem to you a miracle that my life has been extended to the advanced age of forty."

> (They both laugh.)

**ELINOR**

Marianne's romantic soul cannot conceive of anyone over the age of seven and twenty being inspired by passionate affection.

**MRS. DASHWOOD**

You are fortunate to not be above that age, lest Marianne would wonder at your feelings towards…

> (Catches herself before she speaks.)

Forgive me, Elinor, I misspoke myself…I know you have not spoken to me of Edward, although I still hope for you.

### ELINOR
Do not apologize, Mama. I have not spoken to you, because he has not spoken to me.
(Slight smile.)
I need not fear, however. Should nothing come of…Mr. F…I can trust Mrs. Jennings to find me an advantageous match within a fortnight.

(They both laugh.)

### MRS. DASHWOOD
That was wrong of Margaret to encourage Mrs. Jennings. I meant to speak of it to her, but we left Barton Park so late that she was asleep before we turned onto the main road.

### ELINOR
I do believe Marianne meant to speak of it to her on this morning's walk.

(SOUND EFFECT: a loud clap of thunder.)

### MRS. DASHWOOD
If Margaret takes cold from being thoroughly drenched, it will be no more than she deserves. Although I doubt that will occur; she has always been of sound constitution. Unlike Marianne, who loves to walk – no matter what the weather – yet falls dreadfully ill from a trifling chill.

(SOUND EFFECT: a door slamming open off-stage, which increases the sound of rain.)

**MARGARET**
>     (Offstage.)
Mama! Mama! Elinor!
>     (She enters, stumbling and breathing hard. She is
>     wrapped in a cloak. **MRS. DASHWOOD** and
>     **ELINOR** stand. They all speak their next lines
>     over each other.)

**MRS. DASHWOOD**
Margaret! Are you alright? Your clothes are soaked.

**ELNIOR**
Whatever is the matter? Where is Marianne?

**MARGARET**
Marianne is coming…I'm alright… just my cloak is wet…but
she fell…he's carrying her through the garden right now.

**ELINOR**
He? Who is he?

**MRS. DASHWOOD**
Margaret, what are you talking about?

>     (**WILLOUGHBY** enters, carrying
>     **MARIANNE,** who is covered in his riding coat.
>     Ad lib confused exclamations from **MRS.**
>     **DASHWOOD** and **ELINOR.)**

**MRS. DASHWOOD**
Marianne! Oh my!

**MARIANNE**
Do not be alarmed, Mama. I am perfectly alright.

**ELINOR**
(Clears the sofa.)
Here, Sir, set her down on the sofa. Margaret, pray go and get
towels for you and Marianne and this gentleman.

(**MARGARET** exits. **WILLOUGHBY** lays
**MARIANNE** down. General fuss from **MRS.
DASHWOOD** over getting her comfortable
while he talks.)

**WILLOUGHBY**
I was returning from my ride on the hills near Barton Park…

(**MARGARET** enters, hands a towel to
**MARIANNE** and offers one to
**WILLOUGHBY**, who continues the story.)
Thank you…
(Wipes his face.)
…when I came across this young girl running and evidently
upset. I stopped to render what aid I could and she explained that
her sister had stumbled and she was going to get help.

**MARGARET**
We had been caught in the rain and resolved to run for home.
Marianne had the advantage over me…

**MARIANNE**
However, a false step caused me to fall. When I tried to rise, my
ankle pained me and I could not stand…

**MARGARET**
I told Marianne I would go for help and  I ran down the hill.
That's when I came upon this gentleman.

## MRS. DASHWOOD

Sir, we are in your debt. Would you not please be seated near the fire?

## WILLOUGHBY

I thank you, ma'am, but I must decline. I am wet and dirty and would not soil your furniture. If I may have your permission, I would like to call on the morrow to inquire after Miss...

## MRS. DASHWOOD

Dashwood. Marianne Dashwood; and this is my eldest daughter Elinor and my youngest is Margaret. We would be most pleased to have you call, but would you please allow us to know to whom we are obliged?

## WILLOUGHBY

Willoughby; I am presently residing with my aunt at Allenham. Until tomorrow, Mrs. Dashwood, Miss Dashwood, Miss Marianne, Miss Margaret…

(He bows and exits.)

## MARIANNE

(Enthralled as if telling a fairy tale.)

He was like a hero from a story. He rode up and jumped down, removing his riding cloak to shield me from the rain. Then he asked my permission to touch my ankle in order to ascertain whether that there were any broken bones. When he was certain there were not, he picked me up and carried me here as if I weighed no more than a feather.

## ELINOR

Margaret, pray go and ask Cook to heat water for a bath for both of you.

(**MARGARET** exits.)

**MARIANNE**
I do not require a hot bath, I assure you.

**ELINOR**
If you do not get out of those cold, wet clothes, you will catch a cold. I am sure you will not wish to greet Mr. Willoughby tomorrow with sniffles and a red nose.

**MARIANNE**
You are right; I will not. A hot bath sounds wonderful.

(**MRS. DASHWOOD** and **ELINOR** help **MARIANNE** to stand and begin to exit.)

**MARIANNE**
How thankful I am that I have a new dressing gown.

**ELINOR**
It is indeed fortuitous; it was as though you expected to need it for such an important occasion.

(They all laugh as they exit.)

(**BLACKOUT**)

# ACT 1

## Scene 7

**SETTING**:          The parlor at Barton Cottage, the next
                      day.

**AT RISE**:          **SIR JOHN, MRS. DASHWOOD,
                      ELINOR,** and **MARIANNE** are seated.
                      **MARGARET** is reclining on the couch.
                      They are all drinking tea.

**SIR JOHN**
Well, Miss Marianne, you certainly had an adventure fit for any
romance novel. So, Willoughby is back in the country. I will ride
over tomorrow and ask him to dinner on Thursday.

**MRS. DASHWOOD**
You know him then?

**SIR JOHN**
Know him! To be sure I do. Why, he is down here every year.
He's good a fellow as ever lived. A decent shot, and there is no
bolder rider in England.

**MARIANNE**
            (Indignantly.)
Is that all you can say for him? What are his manners on more
intimate acquaintance? What are his pursuits, his talents, and
genius?

**SIR JOHN**
            (Puzzled.)
Upon my soul, I do not know much about him as to all that. But
he is a pleasant, good-humored fellow and has the nicest little
pointing hound I ever saw.

**ELINOR**
But who is he? Where does he come from? Has he another house besides Allenham?

**SIR JOHN**
Willoughby has a pretty little estate in Somersetshire. Allenham is owned by an elderly aunt of his; he is to inherit the property from her.

**MRS. DASHWOOD**
I am glad to find that he is a respectable young man and one whose acquaintance will not be ineligible.

**SIR JOHN**
I remember at a Christmas party at the Park, he danced from eight o-clock til' four without once sitting down.

**MARIANNE**
Did he dance with elegance, with spirit?

**SIR JOHN**
Yes, and he was up again at eight to ride to the hounds.

**MARIANNE**
That is what a young man ought to be. Whatever his pursuits, his eagerness in them should know no moderation and leave him no sense of fatigue.

(**THOMAS** enters.)

**THOMAS**
Colonel Brandon, Ma'am.

(**COLONEL BRANDON** enters, carrying flowers. All, except **MARIANNE** stand. Bows/curtsies.)

### SIR JOHN
Well, Ma'am, I'll be off. I promised Mother I would bring her news of Miss Marianne. Brandon, enjoy your visit with the ladies. Now that Willoughby is back, none of the fairer sex will think of anyone else.

(**SIR JOHN** exits.)

### COLONEL BRANDON
Mrs. Dashwood, I heard of Miss Marianne's accident and come to enquire of her. I thought perhaps some fresh flowers would liven her recovery.

(He hands **MARIANNE** the bouquet of flowers.)

### MARIANNE
(Barely polite.)
Thank you, Colonel.

### MRS. DASHWOOD
How lovely. Margaret, please take these flower to Cook and ask for a vase of water.

### MARGARET
(Takes the flowers from **MARIANNE**.)
These are a vast deal larger than Willoughby's. His bouquet was of wildflowers.

(**MARGARET** exits with the flowers.)

### MARIANNE
I do so adore wildflowers.

### MRS. DASHWOOD
(Trying to cover up the embarrassing moment.)

Mr. Willoughby was kind enough to call this morning to inquire
after Marianne's health. The doctor assures us that it is but a
small sprain and, with a little rest, Marianne should be soon
recovered.

### COLONEL BRANDON
I am glad to hear of it. When you are recovered, Miss Marianne,
I hope to host a gathering at Delaford. I would like to keep my
promise to Miss Margaret to show her my collection of Indian
artifacts. If you are sufficiently recovered, Miss Marianne,
perhaps you would play my pianoforte? I'm sure Sir John and
Mrs. Jennings would be happy to be one of the party; and as well
as Mrs. Jenkin's daughter, who – I understand – is coming for an
extended visit. Delaford, if I say so myself, has a beautiful vista,
although those of Repton's influence might suggest I remove the
avenue of trees.

### MARIANNE
I despise Repton's idea of removing trees and shrubs placed by
Nature in order to make a landscape appear more natural. Only
recall what *Cowper wrote, 'Ye fallen avenues, once more I
mourn your fate unmerited.'

*pronounced "Cooper"*

### COLONEL BRANDON
 I share your sentiments, Miss Dashwood. If the day is fine, I
could have Cook prepare a luncheon and we could picnic.

### MRS. DASHWOOD
It sounds lovely. What think you, girls?

### MARIANNE
Well, I…

### COLONEL BRANDON
I would, of course, include Mr. Willoughby in the invitation, now he is back in the country.

### MARIANNE
A visit to Delaford would be lovely.

### COLONEL BRANDON
As soon as you are recovered, we will set the date.

### (BLACK OUT)

# ACT I

## Scene 8

SETTING:            A parlor at Barton Park, several weeks
                    later.

AT RISE:            **SIR JOHN** and **MRS. JENNINGS** are
                    talking to **MRS. PALMER** and **LUCY
                    STEELE. COLONEL BRANDON,
                    MR. PALMER** and **WILLOUGHBY**
                    are talking. The **BULTER** enters.

### BULTER
Miss Elinor Dashwood and Miss Marianne Dashwood

> (**ELINOR** and **MARIANNE** enter. **SIR JOHN**
> and **MRS. JENNINGS** cross to them.
> Bows/curtsies.)

### SIR JOHN
Ah, my fair cousins.  It's good to see you up and about again,
Miss Marianne.

### MRS. JENNINGS
But where is your mother and Miss Margaret?

### ELINOR
Margaret was not feeling quite the thing today; most likely a
slight cold. Knowing how much Margaret is looking forward to
Colonel's Brandon's  al fresco party, Mama didn't want to take a
chance and believed it was best to confine Margaret to bed. She
asked us to convey her regrets.

### SIR JOHN
There's no need for that; we don't stand on ceremony here.

**MRS. JENNINGS**
My daughter Charlotte, and her husband, Mr. Palmer – along with Charlotte's friend, Lucy Steele - arrived yesterday and are anxious to meet your whole family.

> (**MRS. JENNINGS** turns and gestures to **MRS. PALMER** and **LUCY**. They cross.)

**MRS. JENNINGS**
Charlotte, Lucy, I want you to meet our new neighbors. Miss Dashwood, Miss Marianne, this is my daughter, Charlotte Palmer and her friend, Lucy Steele.

> (All the ladies curtsy and ad lib greetings.)

Over there is Charlotte's husband with Colonel Brandon and Willoughby. I imagine they are speaking of politics or hunting.

> (**WILLOUGHBY** turns and sees **MARIANNE**. He bows to the two men and crosses to the ladies. Bows/curtsies.)

**WILLOUGHBY**
Miss Dashwood, Miss Marianne.
(He takes **MARIANNE'S** hand to kiss it.)
I wondered at the sudden brightness in the room. When I looked up, I realized the source was your beauty.

**MRS. JENNINGS**
Oh la, Willoughby, I vow you spent hours thinking of such a pretty compliment. I am sorry, Charlotte, Miss Steele; Mr. Willoughby would have the world think there is none like Miss Marianne.

**WILLOUGHBY**
I would not wish to offend anyone's sensibilities, but I cannot
speak but the truth.
(To **MARIANNE**.)
If you would care to step on the balcony, I'm certain you will
drive the moon from the night sky.

(**MARIANNE** and **WILLOUGHBY** exit.
**ELINOR** is obviously embarrassed.)

**MRS. JENNINGS**
See, it is as I told Charlotte and Miss Steele; we are all
momentarily expecting an announcement between Miss
Marianne and Willoughby.

**MRS. PALMER**
I see what you mean, Mama.

**LUCY**
The affection they have for each other is quite obvious.

**ELINOR**
Marianne abhors suppression of any passion.

**LUCY**
How fortunate for Miss Marianne and Mr. Willoughby that they
can be so open about their feelings.

**MRS. JENNINGS**
It is refreshing to see a couple so besotted. They are rarely out of
each other's company, although it can be mis-interpreted by
some. Miss Dashwood, I was going to tell your mother, but as
she is not here, I will tell you and trust you to convey it to her. I
was telling Charlotte and Miss Steele about a comment Mrs.
Maxwell made to me yesterday. We met in the village and were
admiring a new hat in the milliner's window, when Miss

Marianne and Willoughby came down the street in his curricle at such a clipping pace. I waved at Miss Marianne and Mrs. Maxwell made some rather disparaging comments about the propriety of Miss Marianne riding with Willoughby un-chaperoned. "In my day," said she, "young women who had a care about their reputation would not be seen thusly." She also conveyed to me that her maid had it on good authority that Miss Marianne had allowed Willoughby to cut a lock of her hair as a remembrance. "I never gave a lock of my hair until after the banns were read," said she. I can assure you, Miss Dashwood, I gave her a sharp set down. Speaking that way about my young friend! Come Charlotte, Miss Steele; I must see about refreshments for our new arrivals.

(**COLONEL BRANDON** crosses and bows to **ELINOR**.)

### COLONEL BRANDON
Miss Dashwood. I had hoped to speak to you and Miss Marianne about tomorrow's outing, but I see that Willoughby has spirited her away.

### ELINOR
Yes, he has, Colonel. Marianne has always been impulsive, and does not approve of hiding her emotions, even if it means setting propriety at naught.

### COLONEL BRANDON
She is merely unspoiled and high-spirited.

### ELINOR
I hope she does not regret her actions. She needs to understand what the world expects of her.

**COLONEL BRANDON**
Miss Dashwood, I knew a lady who reminds me of your sister.
When she was forced into what the world expected of her, the
results were not what one would wish on anyone. Miss Steele, I
understand that you and the Palmers have consented to join the
tomorrow's gathering at Delaford.

**LUCY**
Yes, Colonel Brandon. It was so kind of you to include us in the
invitation.

**COLONEL BRADON**
It was my pleasure. If you ladies will excuse me, I must speak to
Sir John about sufficient conveyances for the outing.
                    (He bows and crosses the room to **SIR JOHN**.)

**LUCY**
 How do you like Devonshire, Miss Dashwood? I suppose you
were very sorry to leave Sussex.

**ELINOR**
 I confess I was, although Mrs. Jennings, Sir John, and Colonel
Brandon are kind and attentive neighbors.

**LUCY**
I am so pleased to have met you, for I heard a vast deal about
you from one who is a mutual acquaintance.

**ELINOR**
Truly? Who?

**LUCY**
Edward Ferrars.

**ELINOR**
You know Mr. Ferrars?

**LUCY**

I met Mr. Ferrars five years ago when he came to Exeter to study under my uncle. He spent four years with my uncle, which afforded us many opportunities to meet. As he was recently traveling through Exeter, he kindly stopped to pay his respects to my uncle. It was then he told us all about you and your mother and sisters. I feel as if I know you already. Indeed, I hope that we may become good friends.

**SIR JOHN**
>           (Speaking to **COLONEL BRANDON** loud
>           enough to be heard by all in the room.)

It's settled then.
>           (To the entire group.)

Brandon and I have arranged everything. We will meet at Delaford in the morning.

**COLONEL BRANDON**

The weather promises to be accommodating, so we will be able to partake of a picnic luncheon.

**LUCY**

It appears we have arrived in time for a most memorable day.

**(BLACKOUT)**

# ACT I

## Scene 9

SETTING:              Outside Delaford the next day.

AT RISE:              **COLONEL BRANDON, MRS.
                      JENNINGS, SIR JOHN, MRS.
                      PALMER, MR. PALMER,
                      LUCY, MRS. DASHWOOD,
                      ELINOR, MARIANNE**, and
                      **MARGARET** are getting ready for the
                      picnic; checking baskets of foods, ad
                      libbing on the weather, who will ride
                      with whom, etc. **MARIANNE** is
                      looking off-stage.

#### MRS. PALMER
I am so glad to have finally met you, Mrs. Dashwood, for my
mama has written such lovely things about you, Mr. Palmer and
I were curious as to whether she was exaggerating, were we not,
Mr. Palmer?

#### MR. PALMER
(Bored.)
I was not.

#### MRS. PALMER
(Laughs as if he made a joke.)
Oh, Mr. Palmer! You must pay him no mind, Mrs. Dashwood.
Mr. Palmer used to be an MP and making everyone like him was
quite fatiguing.

#### MR. PALMER
I never said anything so ridiculous.

**MRS. JENNINGS**
(Uncomfortable laugh.)
Mr. Palmer is so droll today. So, Miss Steele, how do you like
Delaford? For I know you wrote in your last letter that you
wished to see it.

**MRS. PALMER**
Delaford? She wished to meet the Misses Dashwood. She spoke
of nothing else all the way here, is that not so, Mr. Palmer?

> (**MR. PALMER** ignores them. **MRS.
> JENNINGS** tries to cover the awkward
> moment.)

**MRS. JENNINGS**
Well, that is understandable, for they are delightful neighbors. If
their hearts were not already claimed, I have no doubt Miss
Dashwood and Miss Marianne would make advantageous
matches. See how Miss Marianne waits impatiently for
Willoughby to arrive? Once he is here, we will not be able to
squeeze a feather between them. As for Miss Dashwood,
although she will not confess his name, there is the famous Mr…

> (**MRS. DASHWOOD** interrupts **MRS.
> JENNINGS**.)

**MRS. DASHWOOD**
Mrs. Palmer, your mama tells me you and Mr. Palmer have a
young son.

**MRS. PALMER**
We do indeed. Albert is six months old and the sweetest thing.

**MRS. JENNINGS**
He laughs all the time, just like his mama. And so smart…

**MRS. PALMER**
Yes he is. He is already attempting to speak, which I understand
is not common for babes of his age. Whenever he sees Mr.
Palmer, he shapes his sweet little mouth just so...
					(Makes a tiny pursed mouth.)
and says, "Pa!" Now, if that isn't 'Papa' I don't know what it is.
Isn't that so, Mr. Palmer?

**MR. PALMER**
As I know nothing of babes in arms, I am not a competent
reference for your question.

**MRS. PALMER**
					(Laughs.)
Mr. Palmer, if you are not careful, Mrs. Dashwood will think
you care nothing for your first-born son.

**MRS. JENNINGS**
I daresay she will not. Mrs. Dashwood and I understand that men
are not comfortable around babies. Let little Albert grow several
more years and his papa will show some interest in him then,
Charlotte. Ah, here comes Willoughby; now we are all gathered.

					**(WILLOUGHBY** enters and crosses to
					**MARIANNE**. He kisses her hand and
					bows to the assembled group.)

**WILLOUGHBY**
Good morning, one and all. What a fine day we have for our
outing.

					(An **EXPRESS RIDER** enters in a hurry.)

**EXPRESS RIDER**
Which of you gentlemen is Colonel Brandon?

**COLONEL BRANDON**

I am he.

> (The **EXPRESS RIDER** takes a folded letter
> from the inner pocket of his coat and hands it to
> **COLONEL BRANDON. COLONEL
> BRANDON** opens the letter and reads.
> Suddenly he is quite agitated.)

**COLONEL BRANDON**

Prepare my horse immediately.

**SIR JOHN**

What is the matter, Brandon?

**MRS. JENNINGS**

No bad news? Is it about your sister? Is she worse?

**COLONEL BRANDON**

No, ma'am, I thank you, but it is not about my sister. However, it
is imperative that I leave for London immediately.

**SIR JOHN**

Now? Could you not go tomorrow?

**COLONEL BRANDON**

I must leave as soon as my horse is readied, but you should all
stay and enjoy the luncheon Cook prepared.

**MRS. JENNINGS**

We cannot stay at Delaford without our host.

**WILLOUGHBY**

Could you not defer your trip until after our picnic? You would
not be six hours later.

**COLONEL BRANDON**
I cannot afford to lose one hour. Pray, forgive me for ruining our outing; perhaps one day we can plan another picnic. For now…farewell.

>(He bows and exits in a hurry. They all are silent and awkward for a moment.)

**MRS. JENNINGS**
Well, I have never seen Brandon so distraught. I wonder whatever could be the matter?

**MARGARET**
Are we not to picnic?

**MRS. DASHWOOD**
My dear, we cannot picnic at Delaford without our host.

**SIR JOHN**
But we do not have to forego our pleasure, Miss Margaret. We can all go to Barton Park and picnic there.

**MRS. JENNINGS**
That's what we must do, Sir John. Come, let's you and I ride ahead and make plans with Cook.

>(**MRS. JENNINGS** and **SIR JOHN** exit first. The rest follows in groups, with **ELINOR, MARIANNE** and **WILLOUGHBY** following last.)

**ELINOR**
I do hope Colonel Brandon's business isn't serious.

**WILLOUGHBY**
I doubt that it is serious at all, Miss Dashwood.

**ELINOR**
What do you mean?

**WILLOUGHBY**
There are some people who cannot bear a party of pleasure;
Brandon is one of them. I dare say he was afraid of catching cold
and invented this trick for getting out of it. I would lay fifty
guineas the letter was of his own writing.

**ELINOR**
I cannot see the Colonel inventing such a trick as you describe,
Mr. Willoughby. Everybody speaks well of him.

**WILLOUGHBY**
Brandon is just the kind of man, whom everybody speaks well of
and nobody cares about. Whom all are delighted to see and
nobody remembers to talk to.

**ELINOR**
Why should you dislike him?

**WILLOUGHBY**
I do not dislike him. I consider him, on the contrary, as a very
respectable man, who has everybody's good work and nobody's
notice. He has more money than he can spend, more time than he
knows how to employ, and two new coats every year.

**MARIANNE**
Add to which, he has neither genius, tastes, or spirit. His
understanding has no brilliancy, his feelings no ardor, and his
voice no expression.

**ELINOR**

I can only pronounce him to be a sensible man, well-bred well-informed, of gentle address and  - I believe  - possessing an amiable heart.

**WILLOUGHBY**

Miss Dashwood, I have three unanswerable reasons for disliking Colonel Brandon. He has threatened me with rain when I wanted it to be fine. He has found fault with my new curricle and I cannot persuade him to buy my brown mare.

**ELINOR**

You both decide on his imperfections so much in the mass and on the strength of your own imaginations. I am convinced that there are few who would earn your recommendation.

(**ELINOR** exits ahead of them.
**WILLOUGHBY** stops **MARIANNE**.)

**WILLOUGHBY**

Miss Marianne, may I have the privilege of calling upon you in private? There is something I wish to ask.

**MARIANNE**

My mother and sisters are invited to visit with Mrs. Taylor tomorrow morning. I will make some an excuse to stay behind.

**WILLOUGHBY**

Would that I could command time to fly until tomorrow, for all my happiness rests upon that moment.
(Takes her hand and kisses it.)

**(BLACKOUT)**

# ACT I

## Scene 10

SETTING:           The parlor at Barton Cottage, the next
                   day.

AT RISE:           **MARIANNE** is seated, crying
                   hysterically. **WILLOUGHBY** is
                   standing nearby. He is obviously upset,
                   not attempting to comfort **MARIANNE.**
                   **MRS. DASHWOOD, ELINOR**, and
                   **MARGARET** enter.

#### MRS. DASHWOOD
Marianne! Willoughby! Whatever is the matter?

> (**MARIANNE** stands, still crying and leaves the
> room without saying anything.)

#### ELINOR
Margaret, pray ask Cook to prepare a cup of tea for Marianne.

> (**MARGARET** exits.)

#### MRS. DASHWOOD
Mr. Willoughby? Whatever is the matter with Marianne? Is she
ill?

#### WILLOUGHBY
> (With a forced smile.)

I hope not. It is I who may rather expect to be ill – for I am now
suffering under a very heavy disappointment.

#### ELINOR
Disappointment?

**WILLOUGHBY**
Yes, for I am unable to…I mean, I must…Mrs. Smith – my aunt
– has this morning exercised the privilege of riches upon a poor
dependent cousin, by sending me on business to London. I am
now come to take my farewell of you.

**MRS. DASHWOOD**
To London? Are you going this morning?

**WILLOUGHBY**
Almost this moment.

**ELINOR**
Surely Mrs. Smith's business will not detain you from us long.

**WILLOUGHBY**
You are very kind, but I have no idea of returning into
Devonshire immediately. My visits to my aunt are never
repeated within the twelvemonth.

**MRS. DASHWOOD**
Is Mrs. Smith your only friend in the area and Allenham the only
house in the neighborhood to which you will be welcome? Can
you wait for an invitation here?

**WILLOUGHBY**
You are too good…my engagements at present…are of such a
nature…that…I dare not flatter myself.
                    (Pause, then sudden outburst.)
It is folly to linger in this manner. I will not torment myself any
longer by remaining among friends whose society it is
impossible for me now to enjoy.
                    (Gets himself under control.)
Farewell, Mrs. Dashwood, Miss Dashwood. Pray convey my
best to Miss Margaret and Miss Marianne.
                    (Bows and exits.)

**ELINOR**

I wonder what could have happened? Could they have quarreled?

**MRS. DASHWOOD**

I am persuaded that Mrs. Smith suspects Willoughby's regard for Marianne and disapproves of it. Perhaps she has another lady in mind for him and on that account is eager to get him away.

**ELINOR**

His affections today were colder than yesterday and his leave-taken sudden.

**MRS. DASHWOOD**

Elinor, you are resolved to blame him because he took leave of us with less affection than his usual behavior. What is it you suspect him of?

**ELINOR**

I can hardly tell you. Willoughby may undoubtedly have very sufficient reason for his conduct. But it would have been more like Willoughby to acknowledge them at once. Secrecy may be advisable, but still I cannot help wondering at it being practiced by him. It may be proper to conceal their engagement – if they are engaged – but there is no excuse for their concealing it from us.

**MRS. DASHWOOD**

Concealing it from us? This is strange indeed, when your eyes have been reproaching them every day for incautiousness.

**ELINOR**

I want no proof of their affection, but of their engagement.

**MRS. DASHWOOD**
I am perfectly satisfied of both. We must allow Marianne
opportunities to reveal her heart to us.

**ELINOR**
What do you suggest?

**MRS. DASHWOOD**
We are to go to Barton Park tonight for supper and cards tonight.
Mayhap an evening of pleasant diversions will lighten
Marianne's sorrows sufficiently that she will share what
occurred between her and Willoughby.

(SOUND EFFECT: Marianne crying heard off
stage.)

**ELINOR**
(Dry humor.)
I hope so, ma'am, for I know that cards and crab cakes and Mrs.
Jennings' witticisms have the power to remove the sadness of
separation from one you love.

**(BLACKOUT)**

# ACT I

## Scene 11

SETTING:                     The parlor at Barton Park that evening.

AT RISE:                     The group is playing cards. **SIR JOHN,
                             LUCY STEELE, ELINOR** and
                             **MARGARET** are at one table, while
                             **MRS. JENNINGS, MRS.
                             DASHWOOD, MRS. PALMER** and
                             **MR. PALMER** are at another.
                             **MARIANNE** is playing sad tunes on
                             the pianoforte.

### MRS. JENNINGS
How melancholy Devonshire has become, now that Willoughby
and Colonel Brandon are gone.

### MRS. DASHWOOD
We do miss them both

### MRS. PALMER
It is obvious that Miss Marianne feels Willoughby's absence
keenly. I hope she does not waste away pining for him.

(There is a silence from the awkward comment.)

### MR. PALMER
Here now, are we going to talk about Willoughby or play cards?

(Brief ad lib apologies and comments about
playing cards. Their game resumes.)

### MARGARET
I won!

**SIR JOHN**
Trounced us soundly, you did, Miss Margaret!

**MARGARET**
Elinor and Miss Steele are out of counters.

**SIR JOHN**
So the next round is between just you and me.

>(**ELINOR** and **LUCY** lay down their cards on the table and stand)

**ELINOR**
Whilst you two continue the game, Miss Steele and I will console ourselves with a cup of tea.

>(The two ladies cross to the tea table and pour a cup of tea.)

**LUCY**
Miss Dashwood, may I ask you a question?

**ELINOR**
Certainly.

**LUCY**
>(Looks at the other people and then leads **ELINOR** towards two chairs that are set off to the side.)

You will think my question an odd one, I dare say, but pray, are you personally acquainted with your sister-in-law's mother?

**ELINOR**
Mrs. Ferrars? Although I met her briefly at John and Fanny's wedding, I am not 'personally acquainted' with her.

**LUCY**
Ah. Then you cannot tell me what sort of a woman she is.

**ELINOR**
No, I am sorry, but I know nothing of her.

**LUCY**
I am sure you think me very strange to inquire about her in such a way. I assure you, I am not being impertinently curious. There is a reason for my question. And I am sure I should not have the smallest fear of trusting you; indeed, I should be very glad of your advice on an uncomfortable situation I find myself in.

**ELINOR**
Oh, well, I am sure…

**LUCY**
(Interrupts.)
I am certain you will understand when I explain more fully.
(She looks over to make sure the others are not listening.)
Mrs. Ferrars is certainly nothing to me at present…but the time may come – how soon it will come must depend upon herself – when we will be very *intimately* connected.
(Looks down with a shy expression.)

**ELINOR**
Am I correct in understanding that you and Mr. Robert Ferrars are…

**LUCY**
(Interrupts again.)
Oh no…not Mr. Robert Ferrars. I've never met him. I am referring to his elder brother; Mr. Edward Ferrars.

(**ELINOR** looks at **LUCY** with a wide-eyed shock.)

**LUCY**

You may well be surprised, for I daresay that he never dropped
the smallest hint of it to you or any of your family. It is a great
secret; I do not think Mr. Ferrars will be displeased, when he
knows I have trusted you, because I know he has the highest
opinion in the world of all your family, and looks upon yourself
and the other Miss Dashwoods quite as his own sisters.

**ELINOR**
                    (Still shocked but covering it well.)
May…May I ask if your…engagement…is of a long standing?

**LUCY**

We have been engaged these four years.

**ELINOR**

Four years?

**LUCY**

Yes, although our acquaintance is many years. If you recall, I
met him while he was under my uncle's tutelage. It was there
that our engagement was formed. I was very unwilling to enter
into it, as you may imagine, without the knowledge and
approbation of his mother. But I was too young and loved him
too well to be so prudent as I ought to have been. But you must
have seen enough of him, Miss Dashwood to be sensible of how
he is capable of making a woman sincerely attached to him.

**ELINOR**
                    (Absently.)
Certainly…

**LUCY**

I have no doubt of your faithfully keeping this secret, because
you must know of what importance it is to us not to have it reach
his mother.

**ELINOR**
Your secret is safe with me.

**LUCY**
Everything is in such suspense and uncertainty. I see him so seldom; we can hardly meet above twice a year. I am sure I wonder my heart is not quite broken. Edward's love for me has been put to the test - and I confess I am rather of a jealous nature - but I can safely say that he has never given me one moment's alarm.

**MRS. JENNINGS**
> (Has been trying to play cards and overhear the young ladies' conversation.)

What think you, Charlotte? Have Elinor and Lucy been longing for their beaus?

**MRS. PALMER**
I know not, Mama.

**MRS. JENNINGS**
I know not about Miss Steele, but with Colonel Brandon gone for who knows how long and now Willoughby, I am not surprised to see how forlorn Miss Marianne is.

> (**MARIANNE** slams the paino keys for a moment, which draws everyone's attention.)

**MRS. JENNINGS**
> (Rises from the card table and crosses to **ELINOR** and **LUCY**.)

But Charlotte and I have devised the greatest diversion. What say you to accompanying me to London? I'll open my townhouse and we'll attend balls and picnics and ride through the park.

**MRS. PALMER**
Ohhh, Mama; that sounds delightful! Mr. Palmer and I will come
with you.

**LUCY**
London! That sounds wonderful!

**MRS. JENNINGS**
What say you, Miss Dashwood, Miss Marianne?

**ELINOR**
I would dislike leaving Mama and Margaret alone.

**MRS. JENNINGS**
I knew you would say that and spoke to your mother of my ideas
before asking you.
					(Turns to **MRS. DASHWOOD**, who has been
					listening.)
Tell Miss Dashwood what you said.

**MRS. DASHWOOD**
I agree that it is a wonderful idea.

			(**ELINOR** looks at **MARIANNE** for help.)

**MARIANNE**
What of Margaret's education? Her studies cannot be neglected.

**MRS. DASHWOOD**
I will oversee her studies. I daresay I remember French verbs and
grammar and I'm sure I can call upon Sir John for help with
geography and history.

**SIR JOHN**
I would be more than happy to help. It wouldn't hurt me to brush
up my map skills.

**MRS. JENNINGS**

I received a letter from Mrs. Armstrong-Kennedy, my neighbor, who said that she has seen young Willoughby in town recently.

**MARIANNE**

Willoughby!?
                    (Suddenly excited.)
How kind of you to invite us, Mrs. Jennings.

**MRS. JENNINGS**

I thought that piece of news might change your mind. Come, Miss Dashwood, let us strike hands upon the bargain. You young ladies will come to London with me. If I don't get you all married before I am done with you, it shall not be my fault.

**(BLACKOUT)**

**END OF ACT ONE**

# ACT 2

## Scene 1

| | |
|---|---|
| **SETTING:** | Two weeks later. An upstairs parlor in Mrs. Jennings' London townhouse. |
| **AT RISE:** | **ELINOR** is looking out the window, while **MARIANNE** is seated at a desk, writing. |

**ELINOR**
(Looking at a list in her hands.)
We will have to visit a book store soon. I would like to purchase a new atlas for Margaret.

**MARIANNE**
(Absent-minded.)
Hmmmm....

**ELINOR**
(Notices that Marianne isn't paying attention.)
Or we could go to the zoo and select a tiger for her instead.

**MARIANNE**
Whatever you think.

**ELINOR**
Marianne, I wrote home this morning; perhaps you should defer your letter for a day or two.

**MARIANNE**
(Without stopping or looking up.)
I am not writing home.

**ELINOR**

Willoughby again?

**MARIANNE**

Yes, I am writing Willoughby, but I do not understand your comment of 'again.'

**ELINOR**

That is the second letter to him today. And you have written him at least twice a day since we arrived in London two weeks ago.

**MARIANNE**
> (Puts the pen down to fold the letter while talking.)

Since he has not replied nor called upon us, I must assume that he is not receiving my letters.
> (Rings the bell on the table.)

Until I hear from him, I shall continue to write.

> (**JOHNSON** enters and bows.)

**JOHNSON**

Yes, Miss?

> (**MARIANNE** crosses to hand him the folded paper.)

**MARIANNE**

Please see that this is delivered, Johnson.

**JOHNSON**

Yes, Miss.

**MARIANNE**

And please tell the delivery boy to deliver this letter directly into Mr. Willoughby's hands.

**JOHNSON**
Yes, Miss.

> (Glances at **ELINOR** and then bows and exits.
> **MARIANNE** crosses to the window and looks
> out. **ELINOR** crosses to the tea tray and pours a
> cup. She carries it to **MARIANNE**.)

**ELINOR**
Come away from the window, Marianne. You cannot be
expecting a letter. The boy will not have had time to deliver the
letter.

> (**MARIANNE** takes the cup but doesn't turn
> From the window.)

**ELINOR**
Marianne, you truly cannot be expecting a letter.

**MARIANNE**
Yes…a little…not much. He might have received one of my
letters and be on his way here even now.

**ELINOR**
You have no confidence in me, Marianne.

**MARIANNE**
Nay, Elinor, this reproach from you…you who has no
confidence in anyone.

**ELINOR**
Me? Indeed Marianne, I have nothing to tell.

**MARIANNE**
> (Heatedly)
Nor I. Our situations then are alike. We both have nothing to tell.
You because you communicate nothing and I because I conceal
nothing.

(SOUND EFFECT: Doorbell.)

> (**MARIANNE** whirls around to look out the
> window.)

Elinor! There is a horse in front of the house. *He* has come!

> (**MARIANNE** is quite agitated. She crosses
> towards the door, then turns back to sit in a
> chair, then jumps up and turns just as
> **JOHNSON** enters.)

**JOHNSON**
Colonel Brandon.

> (**COLONEL BRANDON** enters immediately
> upon **JOHNSON'S** announcement.
> **MARIANNE**, who was about to embrace
> Willoughby, is startled. She stares at
> **COLONEL BRANDON** for a second, clearly
> disappointed and – without a word – exits.
> **JOHNSON** bows and exits. **ELINOR** is clearly
> embarrassed at her sister's behavior.)

**ELINOR**
Colonel Brandon! How nice to see you again.

> (Bows/curtsey.)

**ELINOR**
Pray be seated. Will you have some tea?

> (They sit. She pours him a cup of tea.)

You must forgive Marianne.

**COLONEL BRANDON**
Miss Dashwood, is your sister ill?

**ELINOR**
          (Awkwardly.)
I believe she is. She has complained of a headache…and low
spirits…and fatigue. She was going to lie down as we are
attending a party this evening.

**COLONEL BRANDON**
I see…
          (Pauses for a moment.)
Are you enjoying London, Miss Dashwood?

**ELINOR**
Yes, indeed. Mrs. Jennings is a most attentive hostess. She has
shown us around town and introduced us to all her friends. And
what about you? Have you been in London since last we saw
you?

**COLONEL BRANDON**
Yes, almost ever since
          (Pauses.)
I understand that your sister's engagement to Mr. Willoughby is
generally known.

**ELINOR**
It cannot be generally known, for her own family does not know
it.

**COLONEL BRANDON**
I beg your pardon, but I had not supposed any secrecy intended,
as they openly correspond and their marriage is universally
talked of by many with whom you are most intimate; Mrs.
Jennings and Mrs. Palmer.

**ELINOR**
(Gentle; trying not to hurt him.)
I see…although Marianne has never informed me of the terms on which they stand, of their mutual affection I have no doubt.

**COLONEL BRANDON**
(Pause. Stands.)
To your sister, I wish all imaginable happiness.
(Pause.)
To Willoughby, that he may endeavor to deserve her.

(**MRS. JENNINGS** and **LUCY** enter.
Bows/curtsies.)

**MRS. JENNINGS**
Ah, Colonel Brandon! Johnson told me you had arrived. How nice to see you again. Well, as you can see, I am come to town with three of my young friends. Miss Dashwood and Miss Steele you see for yourself; and Miss Marianne, which you will not be sorry to hear. But, Colonel, where have you been since we parted? And how does your business go on?

**COLONEL BRANDON**
Pray forgive me. I must go. I just recalled some business I must attend to.

**MRS. JENNINGS**
So soon? Well, don't let us keep you from your affairs. But we will depend upon seeing you more, now that we know you are in town. You need not stand on ceremony with us.

**COLONEL BRANDON**
It would be my pleasure.
(Bows/curtsies. He exits.)

**MRS. JENNINGS**
(Sits and pours some tea for herself and **LUCY**.)
I do not know what Colonel Brandon and Mr. Willoughby will do between them about Miss Marianne. Aye, it is a fine thing to be young and in love. As I hope both of you young ladies will soon find yourself.

(**MARIANNE** enters.)

**MRS. JENNINGS**
Ah, Miss Marianne. I know you will be pleased to learn that Colonel Brandon is in town. Why, you just missed him.

**MARIANNE**
Mrs. Jennings, has the post arrived?

**MRS. JENNINGS**
(Surprised at her rudeness.)
Ah..why, yes. Johnson gave it to me when Miss Steele and I returned from shopping.

**MARIANNE**
Was there a letter for me?

**MRS. JENNINGS**
No, my dear, there was not.

**MARIANNE**
Are you quite certain? No one left a note or letter of any kind?

**MRS. JENNINGS**
I'm afraid not, my dear. But do not worry. I daresay that Willoughby is taking advantage of this beautiful weather and is out shooting with some other gentlemen.

**MARIANNE**
(Brightens.)
I had not thought of that! This weather will keep many
sportsmen out of town today. I hope he returns soon.

**MRS. JENNINGS**
Do not worry, my dear Miss Marianne. I do not think shooting
will keep Willoughby away for long while you are here. I
daresay we shall see him soon.

**(BLACKOUT)**

## ACT 2

### Scene 2

SETTING:              That evening. A London townhouse,
                      where a small party is taking place.

AT RISE:              Several people are present, including
                      **JOHN, FANNY, ROBERT,
                      CHARLOTTE, MR. PALMER** and
                      **WILLOUGHBY**, who is talking **MISS
                      GREY. ELINOR,. MARIANNE,
                      LUCY** and **MRS. JENNINGS** enter.

**MRS. JENNINGS**
Look! There's Charlotte and Mr. Palmer and Colonel Brandon.
Yoo Hoo! Charlotte!

                      (They cross to them, who bow/ curtsies to the
                      Dashwoods.)

**MRS. PALMER**
Ah, Mama! Miss Dashwood. Miss Marianne. Miss Steele. I'm so
glad you've finally come.

**MRS. JENNINGS**
You must tell me who is here. I thought this was to be a small
party, but I vow, everyone in town is in attendance.

**MRS. PALMER**
Well, I have good news for Miss Dashwood and Miss Marianne.
Your brother Mr. John Dashwood and his wife are here, along
with her brother, Mr. Ferrars.

**MARIANNE**
Edward here? I vow, it will be wonderful to see him again, will it not, Elinor?

**MRS. PALMER**
It is not Mr. Edward Ferrars who is here, but Mr. *Robert* Ferrars.

> (**JOHN, FANNY** and **ROBERT** cross to them. Curtsies/bows.)

**JOHN**
Ah, my dear sisters. Marianne, Elinor. I did not know you were in town.

**ELINOR**
We are guests of our friend, Mrs. Jennings. May I introduce you to Mrs. Jennings, Mrs. Palmer, Mr. Palmer, Miss Lucy Steele and Colonel Brandon. This is my brother John Dashwood and his wife.

**FANNY**
And this is my brother, Mr. Robert Ferrars.

> (Ad lib greetings. **MARIANNE** begins looking around the room while the others talk.)

**ROBERT**
> (Slightly snobbish.)

Miss Dashwood, Fanny tells me that you live in a cottage in Devonshire. I am excessively fond of a cottage; there is always so much comfort, so much elegance about them. Some might think there can be no accommodation, no space in a cottage, but that is all a mistake. If people do but know how to set about it, every comfort may be enjoyed in a cottage as in the most spacious dwelling.

**LUCY**
I agree with Mr. Ferrars. If I were to choose, I would be most happy in a cottage.

>(**MARIANNE** grabs **ELINOR'S** arm and pulls her aside. Points at **WILLOUGHBY.**)

**MARIANNE**
Good heavens, Elinor! Willoughby is there! Why does he not look at me?

**ELINOR**
Pray compose yourself, and do not betray what you feel to everybody present.

**MARIANNE**
I care not what everyone thinks. Why does he not come over and speak with me? Willoughby!

>(She crosses to **WILLOUGHBY** who turns and bows.)

**WILLOUGHBY**
Miss Dashwood. Miss Marianne. How are you? How is your mother? Have you been in town long?

**MARIANNE**
For heaven's sake, Willoughby, what is the meaning of this? Have you not received my letters? Will you not shake hands with me?

>(**WILLOUGHBY** is conscious of everyone watching. He takes her hand briefly.)

### MARIANNE

Have you not received my notes? There must be some dreadful mistake. What can be the meaning of it? Tell me, Willoughby, what is the matter?

### WILLOUGHBY
> (Looks at **MISS GREY**, then back at **MARIANNE.**)

I had the pleasure of receiving the information of your arrival in town, which you were so good as to send me. If you will excuse me.

> (He bows and, taking the arm of **MISS GREY** and walks to the other side of the room. **MARIANNE** is nearly faint with anxiety. **ELINOR** crosses to her, takes her arm to support her.)

### MARIANNE

Go to him, Elinor, and force him to come to me. Tell him I must see him again. I must speak with him instantly. I shall not have a moment's peace till this is explained.

### ELINOR
> (Tries to shield her from everyone staring.)

How can it be done? This is not the place for explanations, Marianne. You must wait until tomorrow.

### MARIANNE

I cannot stay a moment longer. The misery is too great. Please take me home, Elinor.
> (She gestures to **MRS. JENNINGS** who crosses to them.)

### MRS. JENNINGS

My dear Miss Marianne, I just saw it all.

**ELINOR**
If you don't mind, Mrs. Jennings, Marianne wants to go home.

**MRS. JENNINGS**
Why, of course, Miss Dashwood. Let me get Miss Steele.
                    (Sees her with **JOHN, FANNY,** and **ROBERT.**
                    Crosses to her.)
Miss Steele, I am sorry to say that Miss Marianne is not feeling
well and we must take her home.

**LUCY**
Oh, I am so sorry. It was so very nice to meet you, Mrs.
Dashwood, Mr. Dashwood, Mr. Ferrars.

                    (Bows/curtsies. **MRS. JENNINGS, ELINOR,**
                    **MARIANNE** and **LUCY** exit.)

**FANNY**
Well, I cannot say I'm surprised at Marianne's behavior tonight.
What must your stepmother be thinking to allow her daughters to
come to town in the company of Mrs. Jennings? I can only hope
that her outrageous behavior does not reflect on you, John.

**JOHN**
Perhaps we should do something for the girls. We could invite
them to stay with us while they are in town. The expense would
be nothing; after all, I promised my father I'd look after them.

**FANNY**
My love, you know I am always ready to pay your sisters any
attention in my power, but I had just determined to ask Miss
Steele to spend a few days with us. She is a very well-behaved
young girl and her uncle did very well by Edward.  We can ask
your sisters some other year.

**ROBERT**

Capital idea, Fanny. Miss Steele is not like other young girls in town. Only recall how she agreed with me about cottages.

**JOHN**

Well, if you think so, my dear. We'll invite my sisters another year.

**(BLACKOUT)**

# ACT 2

## Scene 3

**SETTING:**          The next morning. The upstairs parlor in
                     Mrs. Jennings' townhouse.

**AT RISE:**          **MRS. JENNINGS, ELINOR,** and
                     **MARIANNE** are sitting. **MARIANNE**
                     is on the other side of the room, pale and
                     not listening.

### MRS. JENNINGS
(In a loud whisper to **ELINOR.**)
Upon my word, I never saw a young woman so desperately in
love. Miss Marianne is quite altered. I hope, from the bottom of
my heart, that Willoughby won't keep her waiting much longer.
Pray, when are they to be married?

### ELINOR
(Slight smile.)
Have you really talked yourself into a persuasion of my sister
being engaged to Mr. Willoughby? I must beg that you will not
deceive yourself any longer. I do assure you that nothing would
surprise me more than to hear of their being engaged.

### MRS. JENNINGS
How can you talk so, Miss Dashwood? Don't we all know they
were over head and ears in love from the moment they first met?
Did I not see them together in Devonshire every day?

(**JOHNSON** enters, carrying a small tray.)

### JOHNSON
A letter has arrived for Miss Marianne.

**MRS. JENNINGS**
Thank you, Johnson.

**MRS. JENNINGS**
Ah, there you are my dear. I'm sure it will be to your liking.

>           (**MARIANNE** jumps up, crosses to him, takes
>           the letter and opens it immediately. She reads,
>           then gasps and, shaking her head, staggers to a
>           chair, where she collapses in tears.)

>           (**JOHNSON** bows and exits.)

**MRS. JENNINGS**
Oh my goodness! Whatever could have happened?

**ELINOR**
I know not.

**MRS. JENNINGS**
I will leave you to find out what you may. I will go help Miss
Steele pack for her visit with your brother and his wife.

**ELINOR**
Thank you.

>           (**MRS. JENNINGS** exits. **ELINOR** crosses to
>           **MARIANNE.** She takes her hand and holds it to
>           her cheek. **MARIANNE** bursts into fresh tears
>           and then hands her the letter. **ELINOR** reads it
>           aloud.)

**ELINOR**
"My Dear Madam. I have had the honor of receiving your
letterS, for which I beg to return with my sincere
acknowledgments. I have been so unfortunate as to encourage

you to believe that our acquaintance was more than that of friendship. That I should ever have meant more, you will allow to be impossible when you understand that my affections have been long engaged elsewhere and, in not too many weeks, I hope an engagement will be fulfilled. I return the letters which you have sent, and the lock of hair, which you so obligingly bestowed on me."

I do not know what to say. I am sorry you are grieving, but much as you suffer now, think of what you would have suffered if your engagement had been carried on for months before he chose to put an end to it.

### MARIANNE
Engagement! There has been no engagement.

### ELINOR
No engagement?

### MARIANNE
No, he is not so unworthy as you believe him. He has broken no faith with me.

### ELINOR
But he told you that he loved you?

### MARIANNE
Yes – no – Never in words declared, but it was every day implied. I felt myself solemnly engaged to him.
            (Looks at the letter.)
'The lock of hair which you so obligingly bestowed on me. That is unpardonable, Willoughby! Where was your heart when you wrote those words?

            (She bursts out in tears. **MRS. JENNINGS** enters.)

**MRS. JENNINGS**

How is she, Miss Dashwood? Poor thing! She looks very bad. And no wonder, for I just received a note from Charlotte. It is too true. He is to be married very soon to Miss Grey, that good-for-nothing fellow! Well, all I can say is, he has used my young friend abominably and I wish with all my soul that his wife may plague his heart out.

He is not the only young man in the world worth having, my dear Miss Marianne. With your pretty face you will never want for admirers.

I won't disturb her any longer, but will go out immediately to find something to amuse her. Do you know if she cares for walnuts?

**ELINOR**

I know not.

**MRS. JENNINGS**

Never fear. I will find something. I will tell Cook to prepare a special supper to lift Miss Marianne's spirits…perhaps fish and vegetables will do the trick.

**(BLACKOUT)**

## ACT 2

## Scene 4

SETTING:                    The next morning. The upstairs parlor in
                            Mrs. Jennings' townhouse.

AT RISE:                    **MRS. JENNINGS** and **ELINOR** are
                            having tea.

**MRS. JENNINGS**
How is your sister today, Miss Dashwood?

**ELINOR**
I am afraid she is not much better, Mrs. Jennings. I encouraged
her to have some of the toast and tea you sent up and then she
fell back to sleep.

**MRS. JENNINGS**
I was certain the supper of fish and vegetables would liven her
spirits last evening, but she barely ate a morsel.

**ELINOR**
Marianne has always been of a fragile constitution, Mrs.
Jennings and the least thing will throw off her appetite. Right
now, it's best if she sleeps.

**MRS. JENSKINS**
Then we will allow her to sleep all she requires. Although Miss
Lucy Steele is a sweet girl, I must confess that I am glad she
visiting with your brother and his wife. It prevents us from
having to go out in company.

(**JOHNSON** enters and bows.)

**JOHNSON**
Colonel Brandon, Ma'am.

(**COLONEL BRANDON** enters. The ladies
stand. Curtsies/bows.)

**MRS. JENNINGS**
Ah Colonel, how kind of you to call. I vow, had it been anyone
but you or my dear Charlotte, I would have told Johnson to deny
us.

**COLONEL BRANDON**
Good morning, Mrs. Jennings. Miss Dashwood.

**JOHNSON**
Ma'am, Cook wishes to speak with you concerning the meal.

**MRS. JENNINGS**
If you will excuse me, Colonel, I must go. Cook has been trying
to devise something that will tempt Miss Marianne's appetite. I
vow, if the poor thing does not eat soon, she will waste away to
nothing.

(She exits. **ELINOR** gestures for **COLONEL
BRANDON** to sit.)

**COLONEL BRANDON**
(Quite concerned.)
Is Miss Marianne ill? Has a doctor been called?

**ELINOR**
Mrs. Jennings is a careful hostess. Marianne is not well, but she
is not yet on her death bed. I persuaded her to remain in bed and
rest this morning.

**COLONEL BRANDON**

Perhaps then…what I heard this morning may be…there may be more truth in it than I could believe possible at first.

**ELINOR**

What did you hear?

**COLONEL BRANDON**

That a…certain *gentleman* – whom I knew to be engaged – is in fact…engaged to another.

**ELINOR**

If you mean that Mr. Willoughby is engaged to Miss Grey, then, yes, we do know. We understand that Miss Grey has fifty thousand pounds, which would – in part, at least – offer an explanation.

**COLONEL BRANDON**

It may be so…but Willoughby is capable of…how is your sister receiving the news?

**ELINOR**

Her sufferings have been very severe. I only hope they may be proportionably short. Till yesterday, she never doubted Willoughby's regard.

**COLONEL BRANDON**

I have some information which, I believe, might be a means of giving comfort.

(He pauses.)

**ELINOR**

Please, Colonel, if you have something to tell me that will open Willoughby's character further, pray, let me hear it.

**COLONEL BRANDON**

To be brief; you will recall on the day of our picnic at Delaford, I received a message…no, I must go back further. Do you recall the conversation between us, when I alluded to a young lady I had once know that reminded me of your sister?

**ELINOR**

Yes, I have not forgotten it.

**COLONEL BRANDON**

This lady was named Eliza. She was one of my nearest relations, an orphan from her infancy and under the guardianship of my father. I cannot remember a time when I did not love Eliza and her affection for me – I believe was as fervent as the attachment of your sister to Mr. Willoughby.

Although my father suspected our affection for each other, he decided that she should marry my elder brother. You must understand, Miss Dashwood, Eliza's fortune was large and our estates were much encumbered.

My brother did not deserve her – he did not even care for her – and we secretly determined to elope to Scotland. Alas, her maid betrayed us to my father. I was banished to the house of a relation who lived far away and Eliza was allowed no liberty, until she agreed to marry my brother.

**ELINOR**

Oh my…I never knew.

**COLONEL BRANDON**

Did you not? I often wondered whether Sir John had relayed this story to Mrs. Jennings, who would have had no qualms sharing it with you.

The shock which her marriage had given me was nothing to what I felt when I heard, two years later, of her divorce.

> (He stands and begins pacing. After a moment,
> he returns to **ELINOR.**)

It was nearly three years after this unhappy period before I returned to England. My fist concern was to seek out Eliza, but the search was fruitless and what I did learn was of disastrous affairs.

At last, I found her, it was too late. She was in the last stages of…consumption.

### ELINOR
Oh no! Colonel, how tragic.

### COLONEL BRANDON
I saw her placed in comfortable lodgings and visited her every day during the rest of her short life…I was with her in her last moments. She left to my care, her only child  - a little girl – who was by then three years old. I placed the child in a school and provided for all her cares. When she turned fourteen, I removed her from school and placed her under the care of a respectable woman.

Last February, I received word that she had disappeared.

### ELINOR
Oh no!

### COLONEL BRANDON
I could learn nothing but that she was gone. Then word reached me on the day of the picnic, that she had been found. That was the reason for my leaving Delaford so suddenly. I rushed to her side, only to learn that…a blackguard…had taken advantage of her youth. After much cajoling, she confessed his name to me.

You can only suspect my shock, Miss Dashwood, when I learned that it was…

### ELINOR
> (Gasps, shocked.)

Willoughby?

### COLONEL BRANDON
> (Nods)

He had seduced her and left her promising to return. He did not, nor has he arranged to provide for the child she carried.

### ELINOR

This is beyond everything! Is she still in town?

### COLONEL BRANDON

No, as soon as she recovered from giving birth, I removed her and her child into the country. Miss Dashwood, I believed that your sister had truly secured Willoughby's affections and that is why I said nothing. Please, use your own discretion in communicating to her what I have told you.

And now, I must leave you to attend to your sister. Pray convey to her my wishes for her restored health and should there be anything you require of me, you have but to ask.

### (BLACKOUT)

# ACT 2

## Scene 5

**SETTING:** The next morning. The upstairs parlor in Mrs. Jennings' townhouse.

**AT RISE:** **ELINOR** is seated at the desk, writing. **JOHNSON** enters and bows.

**JOHNSON**
Miss Steele.

(**LUCY** enters; the two ladies curtsey.
**JOHNSON** exits.)

**LUCY**
Oh Miss Dashwood, I heard the news about Mr. Willoughby and came at once to comfort Miss Marianne. How is she?

**ELINOR**
It is kind of you to call. My sister is doing as well as can be expected.

**LUCY**
I feel deeply for her. I know what it is to be separated from one whom you care for; but to learn that person is not deserving of that regard must be difficult indeed. That, I can haply say, I have no experience with. Indeed, I am hopeful of soon being able to declare my affection for Edward to all our friends and family. Since you are my one confidant, I had to come at once to talk to you of my happiness…and of course to ask after Miss Marianne.

**ELINOR**
Oh?

**LUCY**

Yes, for since I have been a guest at your brother and sister-in-law's home – and such kind and generous hosts they are indeed – I have not had the opportunity to meet Edward's mother. Until yesterday. You know how I dreaded the thoughts of seeing her. But the moment I was introduced, there was such an affability in her behavior as should seem to say that she had quite took a fancy to me. Such sweetness and affability; just as with your sister-in-law. Now, I am sure everything will end well. And you, Miss Dashwood, have been the greatest comfort to me.

(**JOHNSON** enters.)

**JOHNSON**

Mr. Ferrars.

        (The ladies stand. **LUCY** moves to a position
        that hides her when **EDWARD** enters. He bows
        to **ELINOR.** She curtsies)

**EDWARD**

Miss Dashwood.

**ELINOR**

Mr. Ferrars, how kind of you to call. I did not know you were in town.

**EDWARD**

I escorted my mother to town yesterday. When I learned from Fanny that you and your sister were in town, I determined to call upon you this morning.

**ELINOR**

How kind.
        (Gestures towards **LUCY.**)

Of course, I understand you are already acquainted with Miss
Lucy Steele.

>            (**EDWARD** sees **LUCY** and is obviously
>            startled, but recovers and bows. She curtsies)

**EDWARD**
Ah…yes, of course. How are you, Miss Steele?

**LUCY**
I am fine, Mr. Ferrars. It is good to see you.

**EDWARD**
My sister, Fanny, has told me that you are staying with her and
John.

**LUCY**
Yes I am. Your sister is the most gracious hostess; always
concerned for my comfort. And yesterday, I had the honor of
meeting your mother.

**EDWARD**
Ah…yes…

>            (**MARIANNE** enters, quite pale yet excited. She
>            crosses and takes his hand.)

**MARIANNE**
Dear Edward! This is a moment of great happiness. Seeing you
here would almost make amends for everything.

**EDWARD**
How are you, Miss Marianne. Have you found London to your
liking?

**MARIANNE**

No, not at all. I expected much pleasure in it, but I have found none. The sight of you, Edward, is the only comfort it has afforded. But don't think of me! Elinor is well, as you can see. That must be enough for us both. How long have you been in town? Why have you not called before?

**EDWARD**

Ah…I confess, I was engaged elsewhere.

**MARIANNE**

Engaged! But what was that, when such friends are to be met?

**LUCY**
(In a cutting tone.)
Perhaps, Miss Marianne, you think young men never stand upon engagements, if they have no mind to keep them.

**MARIANNE**
(Calmly.)
Not so, indeed. For Edward is most fearful of giving pain and the most incapable of being selfish of anybody I know.

(**EDWARD** stands abruptly.)

**EDWARD**

I must go.

**MARIANNE**

What? So soon?

**EDWARD**

I just remembered a commission my mother desired me to carry out.

**LUCY**
> (Stands.)

I must return to your sister's house. Mr. Ferrars, would you be so kind as to escort me there?

**EDWARD**
> (Awkward pause, but has no choice. He bows.)

I would be honored.
> (Bows to **ELINOR** and **MARIANNE**.)

Miss Dashwood, Miss Marianne.

> (**EDWARD** and **LUCY** exit.)

**MARIANNE**

It was good to see Edward again, although he seemed out of sorts. Whatever was Lucy Steele doing staying when she could only see that that Edward came to see you?

**ELINOR**

We were all his friends. It is only natural that he would like to see her as well as ourselves.

**MARIANNE**

I do not understand you, Elinor. From your behavior just now, one would think you do not care for Edward.
> (She exits. **ELINOR** crosses to pick up
> **EDWARD'S** tea cup. She lifts it to her face,
> closes her eyes and breathes in deeply.)

**(BLACKOUT.)**

# ACT 2

## Scene 6

SETTING:              Several days later. The upstairs parlor in
                     Mrs. Jennings' townhouse.

AT RISE:             **ELINOR** is seated at the desk, writing.
                     **MARIANNE** is reading. **MRS.
                     JENNINGS** comes rushing in.

**MRS. JENNINGS**
My dear Miss Dashwood, Miss Marianne.
            (Pauses to catch her breath.)
Have you heard the news?

**ELINOR and MARIANNE**
            (Ad lib.)
"No, ma'am." "What news?" "What is it?"

**MRS. JENNINGS**
I heard it from my dear friend, Mrs. Donovan. The short of it is,
Mr. Edward Ferrars, the very young man I used to joke with you
about, has been engaged above this twelve month to Miss Lucy
Steele. They have kept it a great secret for fear of Mrs. Ferrars.

After the comfortable visit she has had with your brother and his
wife – as well as having met Mrs. Ferrars and believing her to
think affably towards herself – Lucy worked up the courage to
confess the engagement to your sister-in-law.

La! Your sister-in-law flew into such violent hysterics and
scolded poor Lucy and declared she was not welcome in that
house another minute.

Then Mrs. Ferrars sent for Mr. Edward Ferrars and demanded that he deny the engagement, and when he did not, she cut him off without a penny. She sent for her solicitor and settled her entire estate on Mr. Robert Ferrars.

When Mrs. Donovan heard of the situation, she sent word to Lucy Steele to come and stay with her. I must go and comfort poor Lucy.

> (**MRS. JENNINGS** exits. **MARIANNE** turns to **ELINOR.**)

**MARIANNE**
You knew?

> (**ELINOR** nods.)

**MARIANNE**
How long has this been known to you?

**ELINOR**
I have known these four months. When Lucy first came to Barton Park last November, she told me in confidence.

**MARIANNE**
> (Grows impassioned.)
Four months! So calm! So cheerful! Have how you been supported? Why did you not say anything?

**ELINOR**
My promise to Lucy obliged me to be secret. I have often wished to undeceive myself, but without betraying my trust, I never could have convinced you.

**MARIANNE**
I do not understand you! You loved Edward!

**ELINOR**
>(Begins calmly, but grows emotional as she
>continues)

You do not suppose that I have ever felt much. For four months,
Marianne, I have had all this *hanging* on my mind, without being
at liberty to speak of it to a single creature. It was told to me - in
such a manner *forced* on me - by the very person whose prior
engagement ruined all my hopes. I have had her exultation to
listen to again and again. I have known myself divided from
Edward forever.

**MARIANNE**
>(Begins crying.)

Oh Elinor! You have made me hate myself. How barbarous I
have been to you. You, who have been my only comfort.
Because your merit cries out to me, I have been trying to do
away with it.
>(She runs from the room, crying.)

>(**JOHNSON** enters. Bows.)

**JOHNSON**
Colonel Brandon, Miss.

>(**ELINOR** quickly wipes her eyes. **COLONEL**
>**BRANDON** enters. **JOHNSON** exits.
>Bows/curtsies.)

**COLONEL BRANDON**
Miss Dashwood; is something amiss? Is Miss Marianne ill?

**ELINOR**
No, no. Marianne is fine. I am fine. Please, will you sit down?

>(They sit.)

**COLONEL BRANDON**

I saw Mrs. Jennings, who told me of the injustice of your friend Mr. Ferrars has suffered from his family. I understand he has been entirely cast off by them for persevering in his engagement with Miss Lucy Steele. Is it so?

(**ELINOR** nods.)

**COLONEL BRANDON**

The cruelty, the impolitic cruelty of dividing two young people long attached to each other, is terrible.

I understand that he intends to take holy orders. Will you be so good as to tell him that I wish to offer him the living of Delaford?

**ELINOR**

But, Colonel, wouldn't you wish to present this offer to Mr. Ferrars yourself?

**COLONEL BRANDON**

No, I think not. I am not acquainted with Mr. Ferrars. As you are his friend, I feel it would be best coming from you. Will you do this for me?

**ELINOR**

Yes, Colonel, I will.

**COLONEL BRANDON**

Thank you. Now I must go.

(They stand. Curtsies/bows. **COLONEL BRANDON** exits. **ELINOR** sits down, in shock.)

(**BLACKOUT**)

# ACT 2

## Scene 7

**SETTING:**       Several days later. The upstairs parlor in
                   Mrs. Jennings' townhouse.

**AT RISE:**       **ELINOR** and **MRS. JENNINGS** are
                   having tea.

#### ELINOR
I am so grateful to Mr. and Mrs. Palmer for inviting Marianne
and I to stop at their home in Somerset before we travel on to
Barton Cottage.

#### MRS. JENNINGS
Ah, yes; Cleveland is a spacious, beautiful house. Charlotte takes
great pride in their pleasure gardens. At another time, I'm certain
Miss Marianne would enjoy them immensely…How is your
sister doing today?

#### ELINOR
She is better, I thank you. She is anxious to return home and is
upstairs now packing her things.

#### MRS. JENNINGS
I know she will be happy to see your mother and younger sister
again. I am sorry I cannot return with you to Barton Park right
now; I must stay here a little longer until Miss Lucy Steele can
make arrangements to return to her home as well. I have no
concerns for your travels, however; with Colonel Brandon seeing
you from Cleveland to Barton Cottage, I know you will arrive
safely. I have never seen a man so besotted with a young woman,
as Brandon is with Miss Marianne.

(Stands, begins pulling on her gloves.)
Now I must leave you; I must meet with my milliner and then I have several commissions from Sir John that I must fulfill before I can return to Barton.

**ELINOR**
            (She stands and crosses to the desk, which has
            some paper on it.)
I understand. I too, have a list of things to accomplish for Mama before our trip and I still must purchase an atlas for Margaret.

**MRS. JENNINGS**
Then I will see you at luncheon.

            (She exits. **ELINOR** sits down and begins
            writing on the paper. After a moment,
            **JOHNSON** enters.)

**JOHNSON**
Mr. Edward Ferrars.

            (**EDWARD** enters. **JOHNSON** exits.
            Bows/curtsies. **EDWARD** is obviously
            embarrassed.)

**ELINOR**
Thank you for coming, Mr. Ferrars.

**EDWARD**
When I received your note, I could only imagine what you wanted to say to me...what you must think of me...

**ELINOR**
            (Interrupts, speaking faster than normal.)
Mr. Ferrars, I am charged with a most agreeable office. Our friend, Colonel Brandon, has desired me to say that,

understanding you mean to take holy orders, he has the great pleasure of offering you the living at Delaford.

### EDWARD
(Confused.)
Colonel Brandon?!

### ELINOR
Colonel Brandon means it as a testimony of his concern for what has lately passed.

### EDWARD
Colonel Brandon is giving me a living? Can it be possible?

### ELINOR
The unkindness of your own relations has made you astonished to find friendship anywhere.

### EDWARD
No, not to find it in *you;* for I cannot be ignorant that to you, to your goodness, I owe it all.

### ELINOR
You are very much mistaken. I do assure you that you owe it entirely to your own merit and Colonel Brandon's discernment of it. I have had no hand in it.

### EDWARD
Colonel Brandon seems a man of great worth and respectability. All who know him esteem him highly.

### ELINOR
Indeed, I believe you will find him, on further acquaintance, all that you have heard him to be.

**EDWARD**
Colonel Brandon, I think, lodges in St. James' street.

**ELINOR**
Yes, at number 912.

>    (**EDWARD** stands and then **ELINOR** stands.)

**EDWARD**
I must hurry away then, to give him those thanks which you will not allow me to give *you,* and to assure him that he has made me a very – an exceedingly happy man. Good-bye, Miss Dashwood.
>            (bows/curtsies)

**ELINOR**
Good-bye, Mr. Ferrars.

>            (**EDWARD** exits. She stares at the door for a moment and then turns to cross to the down-stage 'window' to watch him leave.)

**ELINOR**
When I see you again…you will be the husband of Lucy.

**(BLACKOUT)**

## ACT 2

### Scene 8

SETTING:                Several days later. The main parlor in
                        Cleveland, the home of Mr. and Mrs.
                        Palmer. (SOUND EFFECTS: storm).

AT RISE:                **ELINOR, COLONEL BRANDON,
                        MR. PALMER,** and **CHARLOTTE**
                        are having tea. **ELINOR** is looking out
                        the downstage 'window.'

#### CHARLOTTE
Goodness! That storm appeared suddenly. Do you see Miss
Marianne approaching? She'll be soaked.

#### ELINOR
No, not yet. I confess I do not know where she could have gone.
She's been out for hours.

#### CHARLOTTE
Please do come and sit down, Miss Dashwood. You'll wear
yourself out going back and forth to the window.

> (**ELINOR** crosses to sit. She picks up her cup of
> tea.)

#### CHARLOTTE
Your sister will be fine, I'm sure of it. A little rain will not harm
her. Walking is healthful exercise and I've never seen anyone to
walk as much as she. By my count, she's been on walks several
times every day since we arrived at Cleveland.

**ELINOR**

I was not concerned until it began raining. Marianne's fondness
for walks belies her true constitution, ma'am. Since she was a
child, whenever she got caught in rain, it generally resulted in
her contracting a cold. Since we were in London, she has not
been careful of her health…

(SOUND EFFECT: Thunder.)

**ELINOR**
(Stands and begins to exit.)
I must get my cape and go look for her.

**COLONEL BRANDON**
(Stands, concerned.)
Let me go and look for her, Miss Dashwood.

**ELINOR**

Oh, Colonel, I hate to ask it of you, but the storm is quite fierce.

**MR. PALMER**
(Stands.)
I'll go with you, Brandon. Two of us can cover more ground.
Charlotte, please have our riding capes brought down, while I
have our horses brought around and get some lanterns.

**CHARLOTTE**
(Stands.)
Yes, dear. I'll have some blankets in an extra riding cape. Miss
Marianne will be soaked to the skin.

(General movement of all characters with ad-lib
about the things to do. During this interchange,
**MARIANNE** stumbles in, unnoticed at first.
She is wet and shivering from fatigue and cold.)

**MARIANNE**
El-el-elinor.

**ELINOR**
Marianne!

**CHARLOTTE/COLONEL BRANDON/MR. PALMER**
(Ad lib.) Miss Marianne! She's wet. She's trembling. She's chilled.

> (Before anyone reaches her, **MARIANNE** faints. Everyone rushes to her. **COLONEL BRANDON** reaches her first and picks her up and carries her to the couch. The following lines are spoken quickly, almost over each other. **MARIANNE** is delirious; she moans and mumbles and occasionally she calls for Willoughby.)

**CHARLOTTE**
> (Exits and returns with a shawl or cape which she throws over **MARIANNE.**)

I'll get Cook to warm a brick to place in Miss Marianne's bed.
> (Begins to exit.)

**ELINOR**
Mrs. Palmer, would you please ask Cook to send up some hot water as well for a bath?

**CHARLOTTE**
> (Pauses.)

Of course. And I'll also have her prepare a broth.

**MR. PALMER**
I'll get the fire built up in her room.

(**ELINOR** feels **MARIANNE'S** head.
**CHARLOTTE** enters.)

**ELINOR**
She feels feverish.

**COLONEL BRANDON**
Feverish?! Palmer, send for the doctor at once!

**MR. PALMER**
Yes, yes of course!
(Exits.)

**CHARLOTTE**
Feverish! Do you mean she might have a putrid infection?! My
baby! Miss Dashwood, you understand; I must remove my baby
at once! I cannot subject him to contagion.

**ELINOR**
Of course. I completely understand.

**CHARLOTTE**
I'll take him to Mr. Palmer's mother. Mr. Palmer! Mr. Palmer!
We must leave today!
(Exits.)

**ELINOR**
Colonel Brandon, would you please help me convey Marianne to
her room? I must get her out of these wet clothes and into a
warm bath as soon as may be.

**COLONEL BRANDON**
Yes, of course.
(He picks **MARIANNE** up and carries her off
stage. **ELINOR** follows.)
(**BLACKOUT.**)

# ACT 2

## Scene 9

SETTING:              A week later. Marianne's bedroom at
                      Cleveland and the hall beyond her room;
                      there is a chair next to the door. The
                      'door' needs to be facing to the side of
                      the stage, so that both the hall and
                      Marianne's bed can be seen.

AT RISE:              **MARIANNE** is in the bed; the
                      **DOCTOR** is examining her. **ELINOR**
                      is holding a basin. The **DOCTOR**
                      washes his hands in the basin and nods
                      to her. **ELINOR** crosses to the door,
                      carrying the basin and enters the hall.
                      **COLONEL BRANDON** is pacing the
                      hall, obviously concerned.

### ELINOR
Colonel Brandon. You should go down for breakfast.

### COLONEL BRANDON
                      (Crosses to her.)
Miss Dashwood. I saw the doctor arrive.

### ELINOR
Yes, he is with Marianne right now.

### COLONEL BRANDON
Miss Dashwood, do not prolong the suspense. What does he say
of Miss Marianne?

### ELINOR
I will not know until he has finished his examination, Colonel.

**COLONEL BRANDON**
Miss Dashwood, what can I do?

**ELINOR**
Do?

**COLONEL BRANDON**
(Frantic)
I am not a doctor, so I may not administer medical treatments. I am not a cook, so I cannot prepare healthful broths. I am not allowed to go near her while she is feverish, so I cannot read to her. All I can do is spend every waking moment, standing in this hall, waiting for some news. Miss Dashwood, if I do not soon have a commission that will aid Miss Marianne, I fear I will go mad!

**ELINOR**
Colonel, in her delirium, Marianne has been calling for our mother. I'm sure Mama's presence will greatly comfort her.

**COLONEL BRANDON**
Of course! It will take several days to ride to Barton Cottage and return with your mother. I will leave at once.

(**COLONEL BRANDON** exits. **ELINOR** sits in the chair and leans against the wall. She rubs her forehead for a moment. After a moment, the door opens and the **DOCTOR** walks out and closes the door. **ELINOR** stands.

**ELINOR**
Doctor, how is my sister?

**DOCTOR**
I am most concerned, Miss Dashwood. When Mr. Palmer called me last week, I was certain this was a light cold and Miss Marianne would soon recover. However, she has only grown

worse. She is delirious, moaning – whether in great pain or in
heartache, I cannot tell. I have tried everything – cordials, teas,
even bleeding her – and yet all my treatments have failed. The
fever is unabated and your sister is now in a heavy stupor. If
something doesn't happen within the next several days, I fear for
the worst. I must go now, but I will check back later tonight.

> **ELINOR**

What should I do?

> **DOCTOR**

I would suggest you send for your mother.

> **ELINOR**

Colonel Brandon is leaving to go and bring her back. Please,
Doctor, what else can be done?

> **DOCTOR**

Pray, Miss Dashwood, pray; for that is your sister's only hope.

> > (He exits. **ELINOR**, stunned, covers her mouth
> > and swallows hard to fight back tears.)

> **ELINOR**

No! No! No! Please, dear Lord, no!
> > (She shakes her head in disbelief and cries out as
> > if in pain. She begins her next lines as she
> > stumbles back into the room to kneel by
> > **MARIANNE'S** bed. Prayer is desperate.)

Do not take her from me! First our father and then I lost…E-E-
Edward! I could not bear losing Marianne. Dear Lord, I'm so
sorry. I'm sorry for my lack of patience with Marianne; she is
young and emotional and I should have loved her more. I'm
sorry for the ill-will I felt towards Willoughby! I'm sorry for
caring for another woman's fiancé. Whatever I have done,

please, please forgive me! Please!  Do not take her. Please! I could not stand to be alone.

**(BLACKOUT)**

## ACT 2

## Scene 10

SETTING:            Several days later. **MARIANNE'S**
                    bedroom and the hall.

AT RISE:            **ELINOR** is sitting, leaning back against
                    the chair, with her eyes closed.

                    (The **DOCTOR** enters, sees **ELINOR**
                    asleep and quietly crosses to the bed. He
                    places a hand on **MARIANNE'S** head
                    and, startled, feels her pulse. He gasps,
                    which wakes **ELINOR.** She rushes to
                    the bed.)

### ELINOR
                (Fearful.)
Doctor! Please do not tell me that she is…

### DOCTOR
                (Interrupts, smiling.)
The fever has broken and she is sleeping peacefully. She will
recover. Thank God!

### ELINOR
                (Covers her mouth and swallows hard. Nods.)
Thank God!

                (SOUND EFFECT: Steps rushing up the stairs.)

### ELINOR
Mama has arrived!

(**ELINOR** rushes to the door as **MRS. DASHWOOD** and **COLONEL BRANDON** enter and cross to the door. **ELINOR** embraces her mother, crying.)

**MRS. DASHWOOD**
Oh no! Pray do not tell me Marianne is…

**ELINOR**
No! The fever has broken. She is going to be alright!

**MRS. DASHWOOD**
Thank God!

(She beings to cry. **MARIANNE** awakens and sees her mother. She weakly extends a hand to her mother.)

**MARIANNE**
Mama.

**MRS. DASHWOOD**
(Enters the room and crosses to the bed to embrace **MARIANNE**.)
Oh, my dear child.

(**ELINOR** follows her mother. **COLONEL BRANDON** stands at the door, watching; obviously relieved, but does not smile. After a moment, he turns to exit. **MARIANNE** sees.)

**MARIANNE**
Colonel Brandon.

(**COLONEL BRANDON** stops and turns back to her.)

**MARIANNE**
Please…do not go.

> (**MARIANNE** smiles at **COLONEL
> BRANDON** and extends her hand to him.
> **COLONEL BRANDON** walks hesitantly into
> the room and approaches the bed. **ELINOR,
> MRS. DASHWOOD**, and the **DOCTOR** step
> away from the bed. He stares at **MARIANNE'S**
> hand, as though unbelieving of what he sees, and
> then – after a moment – takes it. He looks at
> **MARIANNE** and smiles.)

**MARIANNE**
Would…would you…read to me?

**(BLACKOUT)**

## ACT 2

### Scene 11

SETTING:            Several weeks later. The 'park' near
                    Barton Cottage.

AT RISE:            **ELINOR** and **MARIANNE** enter and
                    cross to a position on the side of the
                    stage.

**MARIANNE**
            (Points to a spot in the distance.)
There - on that mound – there I fell; and there I first saw
Willoughby...I am thankful to find that I can look with so little
pain on the spot.

**ELINOR**
Do you regret your feelings for him?

**MARIANNE**
Regret? No. I have done with that, as far as he is concerned. If I
could be satisfied on one point...if I could be assured that he was
not always acting a part, not always deceiving me. You must
understand, I am not wishing him too much good; rather, I wish
his secret reflections may be no more unpleasant than my own.
He will suffer enough in them.

**ELINOR**
Do you compare your conduct with his?

**MARIANNE**
No. I compare it with what it ought to have been. I compare it
with yours.

**ELINOR**

Our situations have borne little resemblance.

**MARIANNE**

They have borne more than our conduct. My illness allowed me
time to reflect. I saw in my own behavior, since the beginning of
my acquaintance with him, an imprudence towards myself and
want of kindness towards others. My illness had been brought on
entirely by such negligence of my own health. Everybody
seemed injured by me. I repaid kindness with ungrateful
contempt, to every common acquaintance I had been insolent
and unjust.

But you, above all, you had been wronged by me.

> (**ELINOR** shakes her head. **ELINOR** and
> **MARIANNE** continue crossing the stage
> towards Barton Cottage. The conversation
> should be timed so they finish before arriving in
> front of the cottage..)

No, Elinor. I and only I knew your heart and its sorrows and yet I
did not extend any compassion that could benefit you. Your
example was before me, but did I imitate your forbearance.
Henceforth my life will be regulated by my faith, by reason, and
by constant employment.

**ELINOR**

Then I must look forward to your giving me pillows embroidered
with passages of Scripture for Christmas.

> (They laugh. and cross to a table set in front of
> the cottage. **MRS. DASHWOOD** is mending
> clothes and **THOMAS** enters, carrying the tea
> tray. He places it on the table.)

**MRS. DASHWOOD**
Thank you, Thomas. Ah, Marianne, Elinor, there you are. You're
back just in time for tea. The day was so beautiful that I thought
we would take our tea out of doors. I thought we would enjoy
those strawberry tarts that Colonel Brandon sent to tempt your
appetite. Not the most romantic gift from a girl's betrothed, but
Margaret is excited.

**ELINOR**
Mama…I think that caring for Marianne's health is a tender and
romantic thing to do.

**MARGARET**
Marianne, after you marry Colonel Brandon, would you please
continue sending these strawberry tarts?

(They all laugh as **ELINOR** and **MARIANNE** sit down.

**MRS. DASHWOOD**
            (She sets her sewing aside to pour tea.)
Thomas, were you able to carry out my commissions in Exeter?

**THOMAS**
Yes, ma'am I did. And I also heard that Mr. Ferrars was married
to Miss Lucy Steele.

            (The ladies all look toward **ELINOR** who is
            obviously upset.)

**MRS. DASHWOOD**
Who told you that Mr. Ferrars was married, Thomas?

**THOMAS**

I see Mrs. Ferrars myself, ma'am, this morning; Miss Steele it was. They was stopping by the New London Inn. I happened to look up as I went by the inn and I saw directly it was Miss Steele. I took off my hat and she knew me and she enquired after you, ma'am, and the young ladies and bid me I should give her compliments.

**MRS. DASHWOOD**

But did she tell you she was married, Thomas?

**THOMAS**

Yes, ma'am. She smiled and said how she had changed her name since she was in these parts and how she was now Mrs. Ferrars. She was always a very affable young lady, so I made free to wish her joy.

**MARIANNE**

Was Mr. Ferrars with her?

**THOMAS**

No, ma'am. Miss Steele – I mean Mrs. Ferrars – explained how her husband had some business to attend to in the area and he had arranged for her to wait for him in a private parlor. She had just stepped outside for a bit of fresh air.

(He bows and exits.)

**MRS. DASHWOOD**

Elinor, my dear child…I'm so sorry.

**ELINOR**
(Trying to recover from her shock.)
No, Mama. We all knew Edward was engaged to Miss Steele. I had assumed we would hear of their nuptials from Sir John or Mrs. Jennings. Like Thomas, I wish them every joy.

(**MARGARET** enters and sits down. **MRS. DASHWOOD** and **MARIANNE** stare at each other, while **ELINOR** stares at her plate. **MARGARET** notices nothing and is the only one who is eating.)

### MARGARET
Elinor if you are not eating, may I have your strawberry tart? Cook said she is not gathering as many strawberries from the garden and these might be the last strawberry tarts of the season. I love strawberry tarts. Marianne, when are you and Colonel Brandon to marry? If you wait until next year, you can serve strawberry tarts at your wedding breakfast.

### MARIANNE
Margaret! Do hush!

### MARGARET
What? I did nothing more than ask Elinor whether she was going to eat her tart.

### MRS. DASHWOOD
Girls! Margaret, you are talking nonsense; please confine your remarks to the weather or your books.

(SOUND EFFECT: Horse approaching.)

### ELINOR
That must be Colonel Brandon. He said he would call today with the new copy of Mr. Wordworth's poems.

(**MARGARET** stands and crosses past the table. She shields her eyes from the 'sun' in order to see better.)

**MARGARET**

Yes, it is the Colonel. No wait; that is not his horse. Who is it?
Edward! It's Edward.

> (She waves towards the side of the stage. **MRS.
> DASHWOOD, ELINOR** and **MARIANNE**
> stare at each other for a moment and then jump
> up. Then they sit down. Then they stand up
> again. **EDWARD** enters and crosses to them.
> Bows/curtsies. He is very nervous and
> awkward.)

**MRS. DASHWOOD**

Mr. Ferrars.

**EDWARD**

Mrs. Dashwood. Miss Dashwood. Miss Marianne. Margaret.

**MRS. DASHWOOD**

We heard you were in the area.

**EDWARD**

You did?

> (**MRS. DASHWOOD** crosses to him and
> extends her hand. He takes it, confused.)

**MRS. DASHWOOD**

I wish you every joy.

**EDWARD**

Oh? Ah…thank you.

> (**MRS. DASHWOOD** gestures for him to sit.
> The all sit. **ELINOR** picks up the sewing her
> mother laid aside and begins working on it.)

**MRS. DASHWOOD**
I understand Mrs. Ferrars is at Exeter?

**EDWARD**
Exeter? No, my mother is in town.

**MRS. DASHWOOD**
I meant to inquire after Mrs. *Edward* Ferrars.

**EDWARD**
Ah…perhaps…you mean, my brother, I mean, Mrs.-Mrs. *Robert* Ferrars.

**MARIANNE**
Mrs. *Robert* Ferrars?

> (All the ladies look at him. **EDWARD** stands and turns to cross a few steps away from the table.)

**EDWARD**
Perhaps you do not know – you may not have heard that my brother is lately married to – to Miss Lucy Steele.

> (**ELINOR** drops the sewing, covers her face and bursts into tears. **EDWARD** turns back, looks only at her, takes a step towards her, stops, looks at the other ladies. **MRS. DASHWOOD** and **MARIANNE** stand. The cross towards the other side of the stage. As they pass **MARGARET**, **MRS. DASHWOOD** grabs her arm and pulls her up to follow them.)

**MARGARET**
Mama? What are you doing? Why are we leaving Elinor and Edward alone? Why is Elinor crying? Can I take my tart?

(**MARIANNE** stops and whispers something
into **MARGARET'S** ear. **MARGARET** listens
and then smiles.)

**MARGARET**
Truly? Edward and Elinor?

(**MRS. DASHWOOD, MARIANNE,** and
**MARGARET** continue crossing the stage.)

**MARGARET**
Do you think they will wait to get married next season so they
may have strawberry tarts at their wedding breakfast?

(They exit. **EDWARD** crosses to **ELINOR** who
is still covering her face, crying.)

**EDWARD**
You must understand. I was quite young when I met Lucy. My
attachment to her was a foolish, idle inclination on my side.
After I left her uncle's care, I began to realize that I didn't truly
care for her. However, when she confessed to Fanny that we had
been engaged these past four years, I could not in all honor deny
it. I had made a promise to her and I was going to stand by it.
When you told me of Colonel Brandon's offer, it appeared to me
a means for fulfilling that promise.

However, when she learned that my mother had cut off all of my
inheritance, Lucy's affection for me began to wane. As she had
been often in Robert's company while she stayed with Fanny; I
suppose it natural that she bestowed her affection on him.

When I received her letter, I realized that, instead of sadness, I
felt…relief. It was then I realized that I had never truly *cared* for
Miss. Steele.

(He kneels next to **ELINOR**, who is still crying.)

I never *loved* her. I have only…always…*loved…you.*

(She looks up at him still crying...yet, smiling. She extends her hand. He takes it, smiling.)

**(BLACKOUT)**

**THE END**

CPSIA information can be obtained at www.ICGtesting.com
Printed in the USA
LVOW080217071211

258186LV00015B/23/P